P9-BJL-905

The Effects of Agriculture and Urbanization
on the Natural Environment :

A Study of Human Impact in Southern Ontario

William C. Mahaney and Frederick Ermuth

geographical monographs
no. 7, 1974

I.S.B.N. *0-919604-21-8*

Department of Geography/Atkinson College/York University,
Toronto/Ontario/Canada M3J 2R7

Copyright © 1975 by William C. Mahaney and Frederick Ermuth.
All rights reserved. PRINTED IN CANADA.

AUGUSTANA LIBRARY
UNIVERSITY OF ALBERTA

To LINDA and CHRISTINE

CONTENTS

TABLES

FIGURES

v

PREFACE

The natural environment in South-Central Ontario is
primarily a product of the Quaternary glaciations which
deposited thin drift sheets on bedrock of Ordovician and
Silurian age. Associated lacustrine, fluvial, and deltaic
deposits can be locally important, and all materials have
been modified by postglacial mass wasting, eolian, weathering,
and revegetation processes. The analysis of a few remaining
stands of deciduous forest, in eastern Toronto, and in the
towns of Markham and Pickering, provides basic information
on the nature of undisturbed landform-soil-forest systems.
The nature and character of sites in natural forests, ecotone
zones, cleared untilled areas, and plowed fields provide
the data for an assessment of the effects of agricultural
practices on Gray-Brown Podzolic and Brown Forest soil systems. Analysis of documentation of historical events, agricultural practices, settlement patterns and urbanization
processes provides a broader view of the human impact on the
natural landscape.

Rock-stratigraphic units consisting of till carry
distinctive soil profiles representative of the age of the
unit and the degree of modification by agricultural practices.
Differences can be seen in field morphology, textural and
organic profiles, clay mineralogy, soil-chemical analyses,
and pesticide residue. Soils were sampled and described
from representative deposits of Leaside Till, and associated
lacustrine sediments. These deposits are largely comprised of
dolomite, limestone, shale, granitic and gneissic lithol-
ogies, in an area of middle-latitude humid microthermal
climate and vegetation, on topographically high and well-
drained sites.

The natural, untilled soils are largely Alfisols
forming on hill summits where thin late-Pleistocene and
Holocene loess buries illuvial argillic horizons comprised
largely of till. The profiles are well-aerated and clay
accumulation in illuvial B horizons reaches 45 percent.
Clay minerals in the parent material are dominated by illite-
montmorillonite which weathers to chlorite, kaolinite and
halloysite in the solum.

This soil-stratigraphic horizon merges with forest
ecotone soils, soils in cleared untilled areas, soils in
tilled areas of second growth, and plowed soils. The types
and sequences of soil horizons remain the same between the
forest, ecotone, and cleared areas, and clay mineral-chemistry

xi

relationships are similar. Soil systems influenced by plowing and application of insecticides and herbicides have higher accumulation of clay in the surface, lower amounts of organic matter, and an overall reduction in the carbon-nitrogen ratio. The data indicate that clay minerals and humus adsorb DDT, DDD, DDE, dieldrin, and atrazine in small quantities, but most toxic materials degrade at a faster rate in plowed soils.

Much of the material in this book is based on data collected in the course of field and laboratory investigations from 1971-1975. The authors are particularly indebted to students in courses on soil morphogenesis and soil laboratory methods who assisted with the field investigations to determine the effects of tillage on natural soils, and to students in urban geography who studied the extent of the effect of settlement and changing land use on the natural environment. We thank R. Alexander, P. Bowden, V. Elchuk, L. Gowland, D. Lepidas, B. McCulloch, D. McWilliams, C. Retchford, K. Smith, P. Stones, and D. Wallace for assistance in the field, and R. Hunn and M. Lavalette for assistance in locating historical documentation.

M.D. Kauffman (Soil Testing Laboratory, Oregon State University) provided the soil chemical analyses, and R. Kihl (INSTAAR, University of Colorado) provided particle-size analyses for four soil profiles. The pesticide residue analyses were completed by H.E. Braun (Provincial Pesticide Residue Testing Laboratory, University of Guelph). L.M. Mahaney assisted with the field and laboratory work, and proofread the entire manuscript. E. Cassalman typed and proofread the manuscript. B.D. Fahey (Guelph University) provided valuable criticism of the book. The illustrations were prepared by G. Berssenbrugge, C. Grounds, and B. Kanarens.

We are grateful to several area farmers for providing access to sites and information regarding local land use. In particular we wish to thank Mr. L. Hollinger, Mr. T.G. McConkey, Mr. J.W. Murison, and Mr. T. Severin. Although many people contributed directly and indirectly in the completion of the study, the authors assume full responsibility for whatever errors or misinterpretations occur in the book.

Research support for the physical and chemical soil analyses was provided by NRC Grant A-9021, a York University Grant-in-Aid for Research, and a grant from the York University President's NRC fund. Publication of this volume was made possible through a bequest from the York University

President's Ad-Hoc Fund.

The authors and publisher wish to thank the following for permission to reprint or modify copyright and/or government materials:

Fig. 1.4, p. 6, from Hewitt, D.F., and Freeman, E.B., 1972, Rocks and Minerals of Ontario: Toronto, Ontario Dept. Mines and Northern Affairs, GC 13, 145 p.

Figs. 1.9, 1.10, 1.11, and 1.12, p. 17, 18, 19 & 20, from Richardson, A.H., 1956, Rouge, Duffin, Highland, Petticoat (RDHP) Conservation Report: Toronto, Ontario Dept. Planning (Ontario Ministry of Natural Resources), Map Supplement.

Fig. 5.1, p. 124, from Metropolitan Toronto Planning Board, 1959, The Official Plan of the Metropolitan Toronto Planning Area: Toronto, Municipality of Metropolitan Toronto, Map Supplement.

Figs. 5.2 and 5.3, p. 125 & 126, from Metropolitan Toronto Planning Board, 1974, Preliminary Impressions of the Urban Structure: to 1971: Toronto, Research and Transportation Divisions, Map Supplement.

Fig. 5.4, p. 130, from COLUC (Central Ontario Lakeshore Urbanized Complex), 1974, Report to the Advisory Committee on Urban and Regional Planning of the Central Ontario Lakeshore Urban Complex Task Force: Toronto, Ontario Government, Map Supplement.

W.C. Mahaney
Frederick Ermuth
Toronto, Canada
May 5, 1975

CHAPTER 1

INTRODUCTION

Soils may be defined as natural, anisentrophic, three-
dimensional systems which form on the land surface from the
action of pedologic processes acting downward on geological
materials. The soil body occupies space, and consists of
horizons of inorganic and organic constituents which have a
particular morphology, chemistry and mineralogy, either similar to or different from the parent material. The factors
used to define the state of the soil system are climate,
biota, topography, parent material, and time, and each factor
leaves a distinct environmental signature in the soil.

The selection of sites on late-Quaternary till and
lacustrine sediment in eastern Toronto, Pickering and Markham, Ontario, allowed analyses of 13 soil profiles at sites
where climate, topography, parent material, and time are
relatively constant (Jenny, 1941, 1961). With biota as the
variable, we assessed the effect of agriculture on natural
soil systems. In addition, we collected, synthesized and
analyzed documentation of historical events, agricultural
methods, settlement and land use patterns to determine the
effect of urbanization processes on the landscape.

Field Area

The field area is located along the north shore of
Lake Ontario in Eastern Toronto, and in the towns of Markham
and Pickering (Fig. 1.1). The till plain adjacent to Lake
Ontario is representative of the topography of a large part
of South-Central Ontario. This consists of undulating ground
moraine, ice-fluted moraine, and drumlins. Lineations in
the till plain surface and orientation of drumlins indicate
that the latest ice flowed north to northwest out of the Lake
Ontario Basin (Fig. 1.2). The entire field area was covered
by waters from Glacial Lake Iroquois, but the till surface
is largely untouched, except where beach and lacustrine sediments were deposited (Coleman, 1932; Karrow, 1967).

The highest elevation in the area is approximately
200 m, the relative relief being 5-15 m, except where streams
have cut to depths of 30-40 m. The till plain grades to the
south towards Lake Ontario where cliffs of 50 to 100 m form
the present shoreline. The shoreline of Lake Ontario is at
75 m.

1

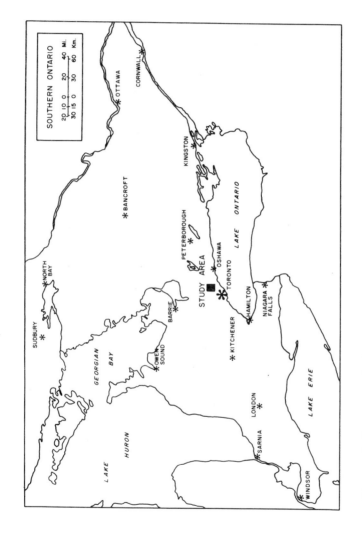

Figure 1.1. Map of the study area.

2

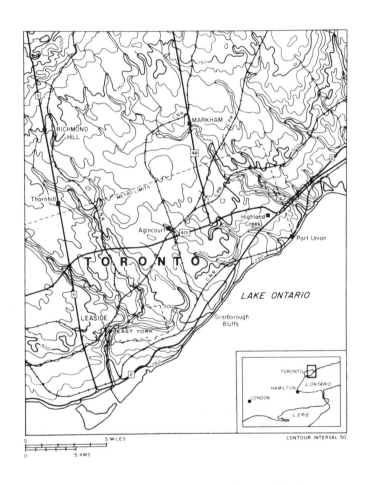

Figure 1.2.   Topographic map of the field area.

3

Streams in the map area drain into Lake Ontario (Fig. 1.3). Most of the valleys are deeply incised to 30-40 m, and this increases closer to the lake. The Highland Creek, Rouge River, Little Rouge Creek, and West Duffin Creek all have some floodplain development as well as from one to three terraces. Soil development on these terrace tracts varies from poorly developed C/Cn Entisols to mature zonal Alfisols with O/A/Bir/Cox/Cn horizons. Profiles range in age from late-Holocene to early-Holocene/late Pleistocene.

Small alluvial fans formed in late-Pleistocene and Holocene time are present in most valleys of the study area. Nearly every terrace tract in major drainages has small fans or cones developed along the break-in-slope between the valley side and the terrace surface. In many cases buried soils are located at the contact along the fan/terrace surface. Although not undertaken for this study, radiometric age-determination of several alluvial fans should provide information on postglacial sequences of erosion and deposition.

Bedrock Geology

The bedrock geology in the field area (Fig. 1.4) consists of a gray to black noncalcareous shale of Ordovician age known as the Whitby Formation (Liberty, 1953, 1955, 1964, and 1967). Quaternary deposits mask most of the bedrock in the area, and the only available information regarding the bedrock surface comes from well logs. The bedrock surface varies in depth from 70 m at the lakeshore to 130 m near Buttonville.

Since all the glacial lobes entered Southern Ontario from the Canadian Shield, Quaternary tills contain between 5 and 20 percent pebbles of Precambrian age. However, the prevailing material was derived from the Palaeozoic calcareous limestones and dolomites; in fact, carbonate rocks make up 50 to 80 percent of the 4 to 64 mm grade-sizes. Shale accounts for only 20 percent of the bedrock outcrop in Southern Ontario, and as a result shale makes up between 10 and 30 percent of the pebble content of tills in the Toronto area. Local exceptions (e.g. York Till) occur where till overlies shale bedrock giving shale pebble counts as high as 80 percent.

Surficial Geology

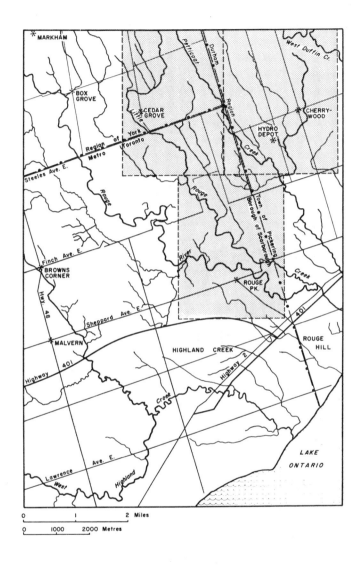

Figure 1.3. Map of the study area showing major
            sampling sites and drainage features.

5

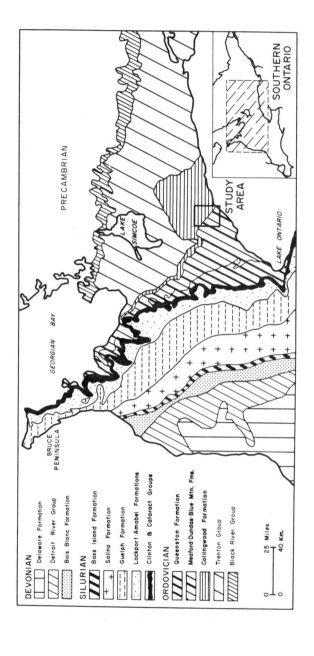

Figure 1.4. Bedrock geology of South-Central Ontario (modified after Hewitt & Freeman, 1964, Fig. 10).

6

The sequence of late-Quaternary deposits in the Toronto area has been investigated by numerous workers (Coleman, 1932; Watt, 1954, 1955; Karrow, 1967; and Terasmae, 1975). Terasmae (1960) gave the name York Till to the thin discontinuous layer of till between bedrock and the Don Formation in the Don Valley brickyard. A somewhat similar deposit of till has been described by Karrow (1967) as occurring between bedrock and the Scarborough Formation in the Rouge River Basin. Here a discontinuous deposit, approximately 1 to 1½ m thick, consisting primarily of shale clasts, and lying unconformably on shale bedrock, is overlain with stratified sand and clay of the Scarborough Formation. This till is considered correlative with that described in the Don Valley brickyard (Watt, 1955), and may be of Illinoian age.

Deposits belonging to the Sangamon Interglacial period are not prevalent in the field area, but various exposures have been described by Coleman (1932) and Terasmae (1960). The Scarborough Formation of early Wisconsin age is found along portions of the Rouge River and West Duffin Creek. Generally, this deposit consists of stratified silt and clay, cross-bedded sand, and massive to irregularly bedded sand. A wood sample from the lower section of the sand member was dated at >50,000 years BP (BGS-230) which agrees with a date of 52,000 years BP (Gro-2555) previously reported by Karrow (1967).

The earliest Wisconsin glacial deposit in the field area is known as the Sunnybrook Till. This unit is usually 5 to 10 m thick, and contains a silt to silty clay texture with a few pebbles and cobbles. The Thorncliffe Formation, located between the earliest Wisconsin till (Sunnybrook Till) and the youngest Wisconsin till (Leaside Till), consists of glacial, lacustrine, and fluvial sediments which are difficult to correlate over long distances. This unit is quite variable in thickness, and in places reaches 50 m. Sediment types range from stratified sand and silt to varved clay. Radiometric ages suggest that the Thorncliffe Formation was deposited between 38,900 ± 1,300 years BP (GSC-271), and 48,800 ± 1,400 years BP (GSC-534) (Karrow, 1967). Two late-Wisconsin tills, the Seminary and Meadowcliffe, have been named from type sections in the Scarborough Bluffs, and are characteristically thin, discontinuous, and difficult to trace over long distances. Probably both tills represent minor readvances of the ice occurring prior to the last major Wisconsin advance which deposited the Leaside Till.

The Leaside Till is named from the type section in

the Leaside railway cut (Fig. 1.5) (Coleman, 1932). This is the uppermost till sheet in the area, and makes up the surface material in most localities where it usually over-lies stratified sand and clay of the Thorncliffe Formation. This till sheet averages 15 to 20 m in thickness, and in places textural changes indicate the possibility of two till sheets separated by stratified sand and gravel. Dreimanis and Terasmae (1958) provide data which show the upper unit higher in shale and lower in dolomite than the lowermost unit. Ostry (1962) described a fabric that was consistently northwest-southeast, while Dreimanis and Terasmae (1958) showed various preferred orientations of large stones for the lower unit and a northwest orientation for the upper unit. Analysis of 13 samples of Leaside Till, including the type section, will be presented and discussed in Chapters 2, 3 and 4. The location of sites in the Rouge River, Little Rouge Creek, and West Duffin Creek basins are shown in Figs. 1.6, 1.7, and 1.8.

The research literature on podzolic soils is reviewed by Stobbe and Wright (1959), Stobbe (1961) and Rode (1970), while investigations in South-Central Ontario are contained in county soil surveys (Hoffman and Richards, 1955; Olding, Wicklund, and Richards, 1956). The soil distributions in the Province are summarized by Richards (1961).

Climate

The study area lies in the humid continental, cool summer, no dry season climatic region of Canada (Brown, 1968). The average temperature ranges from 20°C in July to -7°C in January, but extremes are recorded as high as 40°C in July and as low as -34°C in February. The mean annual frost-free period lasts for about 150 days from mid-May to early October. However, minimum frost-free periods have been recorded as low as 100 days, while the maximum period is recorded at 173 days. Along the shoreline of Lake Ontario, the frost-free period may exceed that of inland locations in the study area by as much as two weeks.

The field area is subjected to the frequent clashes of high and low pressure systems. Outbreaks of cold, stable air masses from the Arctic usually bring clear, cold days and unexpected spring and fall frosts. Mild or warm sunny weather commonly occurs with high pressure systems from the Pacific Ocean, and southwestern U.S., whereas skies tend to

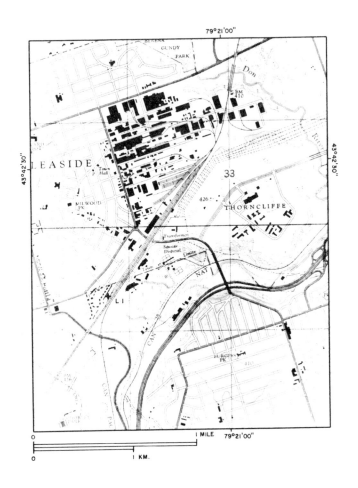

Figure 1.5. Topographic map showing the location
of the type Leaside Till and site L1.

9

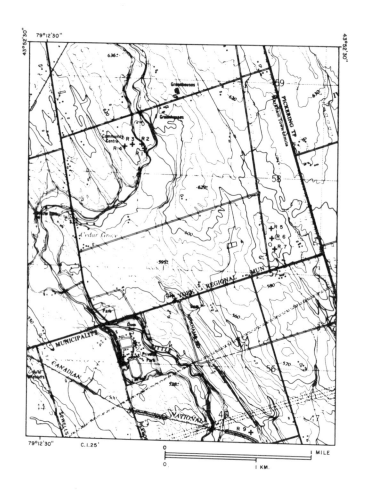

Figure 1.6.   Topographic map showing sites R1,
              R2, R3, R4, R5, R6, and R7
              (Highland Creek quadrangle 1:25,000).

10

Figure 1.7.   Topographic map showing sites R8,
               R9, and R10 (Highland Creek
               quadrangle, 1:25,000).

11

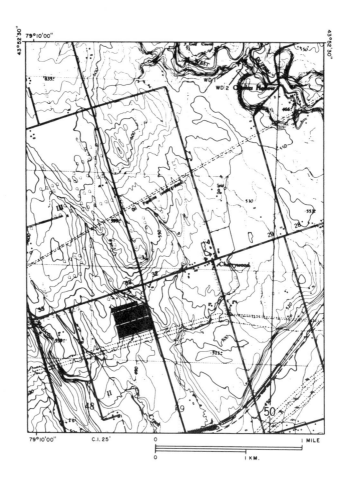

Figure 1.8.   Topographic map showing sites WD1 and
              WD2 (Highland Creek quadrangle,
              1:25,000).

be cloudy when the source region is the Gulf of Mexico.
Tropical air occasionally reaches the area in the summer
bringing with it high temperatures and humidity. Thunder-
storms are common in summer (Brown, 1968).

     Precipitation in the study area is influenced by the
dominant westerly winds, and by the topography. The mean

12

annual precipitation is 850 mm. The lowest precipitation occurs during the winter months from December through March. The mean annual snowfall is 1,650 mm, which reduces to 165 mm of water. The mean annual number of rainy days is 125.

Table 1.1 summarizes additional relevant climatic characteristics of the study area. The data are based on 30 to 50 years of record (Brown, 1968, p. 48; and Phillips and McCulloch, 1972).

Vegetation

In little more than a century Southern Ontario has been transformed from an area of virgin forest into an agricultural and industrial region. The early settlers regarded the forest as an enemy that occupied the lands they required for farms and urban settlements, and which also formed a physical barrier between isolated towns. The abundance of wood and scarcity of markets led to the belief that the supply of wood was inexhaustible. These attitudes, so inimical to forestry, persisted until recent times and, even now, have not completely disappeared (Regional Municipality of York, 1974).

Forests, mainly in the form of farm woodlots, now cover only a small portion of Southern Ontario, and in many places, are so reduced in size that they no longer provide many of the natural advantages associated with tree cover. The process of deterioration in natural woodland cover usually followed the same pattern; forests were cleared for the expansion of agriculture, the exploitation of other resources (e.g. sand and gravel), and urbanization. The remaining forests were progressively degraded through unwise cutting, excessive grazing, and fires.

Table 1.2 shows the remaining woodland as a percentage of total land area in the three municipalities which the study area covers. Although slight irregularities appear in the table, due to incomplete information, the general trend is apparent. Until about 1911, the decrease in woodland was rapid. After that the small remaining area of woodland was at least tolerated, and in some cases has shown a slight increase.

The composition of trees in a woodlot is determined largely by its history, the climate, moisture regime and

13

Table 1.1. Climatic characteristics of the study area.[ab]

Mean Annual Temperature	7
Mean Daily Maximum Temperature	
-January	- 2
-April	10
-July	26
-October	14
Mean Daily Minimum Temperature	
-January	-10
-April	1
-July	15
-October	4
Daily Range of Temperature	
-January	9
-July	11
Extreme Low Temperature	-34
Extreme High Temperature	40
Mean Date of Last Frost in Spring	May 12
Mean Date of First Frost in Fall	October 8
Mean Annual Frost Free Period (days)	150
Start of Growing Season	April 12
End of Growing Season	November 3
Mean Annual Length of Growing Season	205
Mean Annual Growing Degree-Days	3500
Mean Annual Precipitation	86
Mean Annual Snowfall	165
Mean Annual Potential	
Evapotranspiration	61
Mean Annual Potential	
Evapotranspiration	53
Mean Annual Moisture Deficiency	8
Mean Annual Water Surplus	33

---

[a]Most data in this table are based on 30 to 50 years of record (Brown, 1968, p. 48; Phillips and McCulloch, 1972).

[b]precipitation is in cm; temperature in ^{o}C.

soil type. Woodlots within the study area lie near the
northern limits of the deciduous forest region (Rowe, 1972).
This region extends northward into the study area largely
as a result of the moderating climatic effect of Lake Ontario.

Table 1.2.   Woodland as percentage of total land use.

Township	1851	1861	1891	1911	1921	1931	1941	1951
Markham[a]	42.7	31.6	8.9	5.4	3.6	4.0	4.1	3.9
Pickering[a]	45.0	32.9	8.4	3.9	6.1	6.0	6.6	7.3
Scarborough[a]	73.2	33.6	8.3	7.2	6.5	6.7	4.2	7.5

[a] Study area straddles these municipalities (Richardson, 1956).

According to Walden and Griffiths (1974) this forest
region contains the richest fauna and flora of any part of
Ontario. The upland climax association in the study area
consists of the sugar-maple-beech complex and associated
species, such as basswood, white elm, yellow birch, white
ash, hemlock and white pine. The climax association of lowland areas is white cedar, which is the most common forest
cover type in the study area, and the dominant association
in the bottomlands of river valleys. These climax types are
best suited to maintain themselves permanently under the
climatic, soil, drainage, and topographic conditions in the
study area. Unless disturbed by fire, axe, or human occupance they will eventually take possession and hold most of
the area against the competition of other trees. The deciduous forest region is characterized by the presence of
southern species, such as red mulberry, black walnut, blue
beech, black locust, butternut, ironwood, and others (Walden
and Griffiths, 1974, p.16).

A complete survey of woodland for the study area is
contained in the Rouge, Duffin, Highland Petticoat (RDHP)
Conservation Report (Richardson, 1956). A subsequent vegetation survey by Walden and Griffiths (1974) includes only
the northernmost parts of the study area. Relatively few
changes were observed between the two surveys, no doubt,
because mature woodlots are comparatively stable systems

15

which are unlikely to exhibit rapid shifts in their biotic composition.

The RDHP survey (Richardson, 1956) used a slightly modified form of the system drawn up by the Society of American Foresters to classify the forest cover types. The survey does not carry implications as to whether these types are temporary or permanent. The following discussion is based on this survey.

Although 19 forest cover types exist in the study area, about 80 percent of the woodland acreage is contained within five cover types (Figs. 1.9, 1.10, 1.11 and 1.12). The gaps in the numerical system are due to the fact that certain cover types common to the eastern U.S. do not occur in the study area. These types are discussed below in descending order according to the area covered.

White cedar (Type 24) occurs most commonly on the muck soils of the swamps where it has such associates as black ash, white elm, tamarack, red maple, black spruce, yellow birch, hemlock, white pine and white birch. Where lime is plentiful white cedar may extend even to the droughty upland slopes where it tends to form pure stands. White cedar occupies just over 25 percent of the woodland acreage.

Sugar maple (Type 14) originally covered most of the upland or better drained portions of the study area, except the dry sandy sections and those areas covered by the closely related Type 56 (beech, sugar maple). Since this type occupied land which was considered fertile, and with good moisture conditions, much of it was cleared to make way for agriculture. Common associates are white elm, white ash, basswood, black cherry, and hemlock, with butternut, yellow birch, and rock elm typically occurring in the lowland locations. Sugar maple occupies just under 25 percent of the woodland acreage.

Beech and sugar maple (Type 57) is regarded as the typical association forming the climax type for the uplands of the study area. Its associates are hemlock, white elm, basswood, white ash, and black cherry. While this type was formerly very extensive in Southern Ontario, its area has been significantly depleted because it occupied the best land. Beech and sugar maple occupy just over 10 percent of the woodland acreage.

16

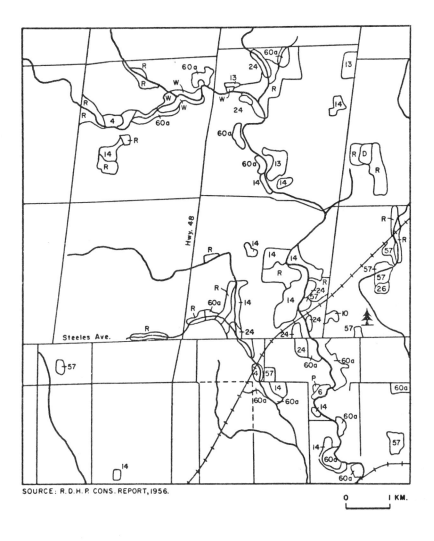

SOURCE: R.D.H.P. CONS. REPORT, 1956.

0   I KM.

Figure 1.9.   Forest cover types, northwest
quadrant of the study area (Richardson,
1956). For legend see p. 21.

17

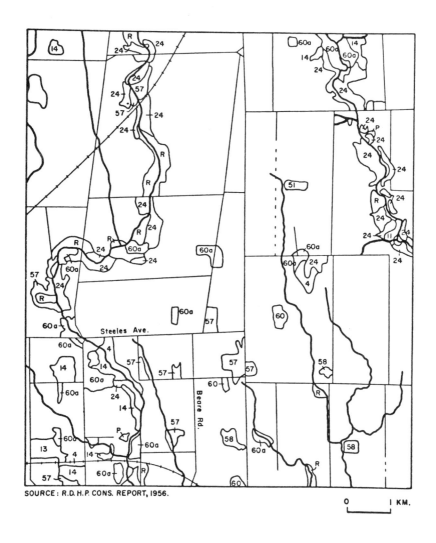

SOURCE: R.D. H.P. CONS. REPORT, 1956.

0   I KM.

Figure 1.10.   Forest cover types, northeast
                quadrant of the study area (Richardson,
                1956). For legend see p. 21.

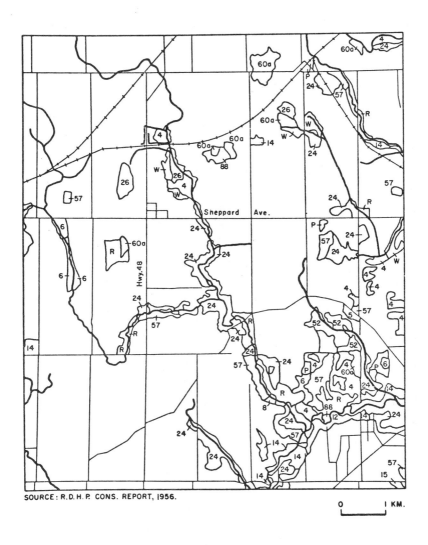

SOURCE: R.D.H.P. CONS. REPORT, 1956.

0   I KM.

Figure 1.11.   Forest cover types, southwest
quadrant of the study area (Richardson,
1956). For legend see p. 21.

19

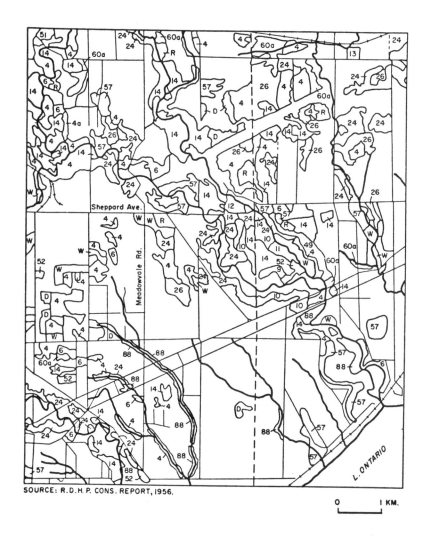

SOURCE: R.D.H.P. CONS. REPORT, 1956.

Figure 1.12. Forest cover types, southeast quadrant of the study area (Richardson, 1956). For legend see p. 21.

R   RECOMMENDED FOR
PRIVATE REFORESTATION

P   PLANTATION

W or D   WET or DRY SHRUB LAND

RECOMMENDED AS
WOODLOT IMPROVEMENT PROJECT

NUMERALS INDICATE FOREST COVER TYPE, AS FOLLOWS:

4	ASPEN	24	WHITE CEDAR
5	PIN CHERRY	26	BLACK ASH – WHITE ELM – RED MAPLE
6	PAPER BIRCH	51	RED OAK – BASSWOOD – WHITE ASH
8	WHITE PINE – RED OAK – WHITE ASH	52	RED OAK
10	WHITE PINE – HEMLOCK	57	BEECH – SUGAR MAPLE
11	HEMLOCK	58	BEECH
12	SUGAR MAPLE – BEECH – YELLOW BIRCH	60	SILVER MAPLE – WHITE ELM
13	SUGAR MAPLE – BASSWOOD	60a	WHITE ELM
14	SUGAR MAPLE	88	WILLOW
15	YELLOW BIRCH		

21

White elm (Type 60a) is quite similar to the silver maple and white elm swamp type, but often occurs on somewhat drier sites. White elm occupies about 10 percent of the woodland acreage.

Aspen (Type 4) is a pioneer type that takes over after clearing operations, overgrazing and/or fire. It frequently is the invasion species on abandoned fields and pastures. It grows well on soils that are wet during a good part of the year, as well as on dry soils. Found in association with balsam, poplar, red cherry, white elm, and paper birch, aspen occupies about 10 percent of the woodland acreage.

The remaining fourteen cover types are present in the study area in amounts which vary from 3 percent of the woodland to trace amounts of only a few acres.

In summary, the upland areas of the study area are generally characterized by sugar maple and beech and sugar maple stands which are the common climax type for the deciduous forest region in Ontario. These types once extended over most of the uplands, but were largely cleared because they occupied the most desirable agricultural land. Both types make up about 35 percent of the total woodland in the study area. The other common types, with the exception of aspen, are characteristic of swamp areas. White cedar and elm grow on lands considered valuable for other uses (e.g. water storage). The other fourteen cover types occupying the remaining 20 percent of the forest cover indicate the great variety of local climatic, topographic, and soil conditions found in the study area.

Methods

The methods employed in this study follow the standard analytical procedures of the U.S.D.A., Soil Conservation Service (Soil Survey Staff, 1951, 1960), with the exception of the particle-size analysis which follows the Wentworth scale (Folk, 1968). Particle-size determinations are calculated after dry sieving for coarse grades (e.g. 64mm-63μ) (Day, 1965), and by sedimentation for fine grades (e.g. <63μ) (Bouyoucos, 1962). After separation of the clay grade by sedimentation (<1.95μ), an air-dried coat was X-rayed following methods established by Whittig (1965), Grim (1968), Birkeland (1969), and Mahaney (1974). Clay minerals were analyzed on a Toshiba ADG-301H diffractometer with Ni-filtered CuKα radiation.

The soil reaction was obtained from a 1:1 soil paste by glass electrode, and organic matter by the Walkley-Black method (Walkley and Black, 1934). Total nitrogen was analyzed by the Kjeldahl method outlined by Bremner (1965). Exchangeable bases and total cation exchange capacity was measured by ammonium acetate methods (Peech, et. al. 1947; Schollenberger and Simon, 1945). Total soluble salts were measured by electrical conductivity (Bower and Wilcox, 1965), exchangeable hydrogen by the Triethanolamine method (Olsen and Dean, 1965), and free iron oxide by the sodium dithionite-citrate method (Mehra and Jackson, 1960). Organochloride herbicides and insecticides were analyzed by gas chromatograph.

CHAPTER 2

NATURAL SOIL SYSTEMS

Important information bearing on the nature of the
natural environment may be deduced from an investigation of
soils forming on glacial deposits under deciduous forest in
Southern Ontario. For example, the effects of agriculture
and forest clearing activity can be determined from soil
morphological, physical, mineralogical, and chemical data.
The state of the soil system varies with the degree of dis-
turbance and provides a useful means of assessing the human
impact on the landscape.

Natural soils, like natural vegetation, are subject
to a certain amount of interpretation. Some workers have
maintained that the vegetation and soils of North America
could be considered as natural when the first Europeans ap-
peared in the 16th through the 19th centuries. Still other
workers advocate that pre-historic Indians exerted a profound
disrupting influence on vegetation patterns (Kuchler, 1964)
and existing soil distributions prior to the arrival of the
Europeans. According to Heidenreich (1963), the area of
Southern Ontario adjacent to Lake Ontario was primarily a
buffer zone between the Iroquois and Hurons, and probably
was not appreciably disturbed by Indian occupance (a discussion of Indian agriculture is contained in Chapter 5).
The assemblage of maple, beech, ash, cedar, and birch as
principal forest species is illustrated in Figs. 2.1, 2.2,
and 2.3. While the vegetation has been modified by selective
cutting on the part of farmers, soils in existing woodlots
do not appear to have been appreciably affected by prehistoric
or historic man.

Soil Morphology

Soil profiles were studied in the Don River Valley,
and Rouge River and West Duffin Creek drainage basins (Fig.
2.4, 2.5, 2.6, and 2.7), and representative samples were
collected for laboratory study (Table 2.1). Each soil is
described as a soil stratigraphic unit (e.g. of post-Leaside
age, ~12,500 years BP), and defined by its stratigraphic
position and those physical features which permit constant
recognition and field mapping. Soil stratigraphic units form,
in situ, from geological deposits by pedologic processes which
act downward. Soils are assigned informal names coinciding

25

Figure 2.1. Site R7, Little Rouge Creek Drainage Basin, Highland Creek quadrangel (1:25,000). The species composition is maple, beech and ash. For location see Fig. 1.6.

26

Leaside Till

Scarborough Fm

Figure 2.2. Site R8, Rouge River, Highland Creek
quadrangle, (1:25,000). The Scarborough
Formation underlies Leaside Till. For
location see Fig. 1.7.

Leaside Till

Thorncliffe
Fm

Figure 2.3. Sites WD1 and WD2, West Duffin Creek, Highland Creek quadrangle
(1:25,000). Leaside Till and Iroquois sand overlie the Thorncliffe
Formation (right); stream terraces of Holocene age are overlain by
alluvial fans and debris-slide material. For location see Fig. 1.8.

28

with the deposit on which they formed (but with the prefix
"post" to avoid a terminologic proliferation).

Soil properties of use in this study include depth
of weathering, horizon development, color, texture, structure,
consistence, plasticity, and stickiness (Figs. 2.4, 2.5, 2.6,
and 2.7). Soil profiles are well-developed on deposits of
Leaside Till, and consist of an O/A/B/Cox/Cn horizon sequence.
The O horizon component ranges from 2.5 to 6 cm, while A
horizons are 15 to 30.5 cm thick. B horizons are 20 to 38
cm thick, and display either iron oxide coats on peds (ir)
or increased clay accumulation (t) usually accompanied by
clay skins. C horizons range from 38 to 80 cm. Total depth
of soil ranges from 89 to 114 cm. The soil at the type
Leaside (site L1), is only 61 cm, and lacks a B horizon.

O1
A1
A2
B2t
Cmox
Cn

Figure 2.4. Soil profile R6. For location see Fig.
1.6. The mattock is 68 cm.

29

O1
A1
B2ir

C1ox

C2mox

Cnm

Figure 2.5.   Soil profile R7.   For location see Fig.
1.6.   The mattock is 68 cm.

OI
AII
AI2

B2ir

CIox

C2ox

Cn

Figure 2.6.   Soil profile R8.   For location see Fig.
1.7.   The mattock is 68 cm.

Ol
All
Al2

B2t

Cox

Cn

Figure 2.7. Soil profile R10. For location see Fig.
1.7. The mattock is 68 cm.

Surface colors (0 horizons) are black (10YR 2/1 to
10YR 1/1). A horizons are lighter in hue and range from
black (10YR 2/1) to brownish-black (10YR 2/3, 10YR 3/2),
brownish-gray (10YR 4/1), brown (10YR 4/4), dull yellowish-
brown (10YR 5/3), grayish-yellow brown (10YR 5/2), and dull
yellow orange (10YR 6/3). B horizons vary from dark brown
(10YR 3/4), to mottled brown (10YR 4/6), dull yellowish-
brown (10YR 5/4), brown (10YR 4/4, 10YR 4/6), light yellow
(2.5Y 7/4), and dull yellow orange (10YR 6/4). C horizons
have drab and often mottled colors which range from dark
brown (10YR 3/3) to brown (10YR 4/4), dull yellow orange
(10YR 6/3, 10YR 7/2), dull reddish-brown (5YR 4/4), light
yellow (2.5Y 7/3), and grayish-yellow (2.5Y 7/2). Parent
materials (Cn) are usually grayish-yellow (2.5Y 7/2, 6/2),
dull yellow (2.5Y 6/4), yellowish-brown (2.5Y 5/4), light
yellow (2.5Y 7/3), and/or light yellow (5Y 7/3).

A horizon textures vary from loam and pebbly loam to
sandy loam. B horizons have clay loam, loam, and sandy loam
textures with slightly higher percentages of clay. C horizons
have pebbly sandy loam, pebbly loamy sand, pebbly loam, pebbly
silty clay loam, and clay textures. Structures in the A
horizons are generally granular, while B horizons are weak
to well-developed blocky, and C horizons are weak blocky to
massive. Moist consistencies in the A horizons are usually
friable to firm, B horizons are friable to very firm, and
C horizons are loose to very firm depending on the amount of
clay present. Unconfined shear strengths give average values
(n=40) of 1.1 kg/cm^2 in the A horizons. B horizons (n=40)
yield values of 2.0, and C horizons (n=80) average 4.2.

The subsurface horizons in many post-Leaside soils
show strongly differentiated mottling, possibly a result of
alternate oxidation and reduction in response to fluctuating
water tables and/or poor leaching effects in the soil systems.
The undulatory nature of many surface horizon contacts and
irregular surface microrelief may result from seasonal frost
heaving, particularly in snow-free and poorly vegetated areas
where frost penetration into the solum is more rapid.

Particle Size

The coarse grade-sizes (64-2 mm) are dominated by large
to medium pebbles (Table 2.2). Sand, silt, and clay dominate
over pebbles and granules with the <2 mm fractions accounting
for 90 percent of the total sample. Within the <2 mm fractions
sand and silt dominate over clay. Generally the A and B

Table 2.1. Relict soil profiles[a,b] from stands of mixed-hardwood forest.

Profile: L1

Age: post-Leaside

Location: Leaside Cut, west side of the Don River Valley, type Leaside.

Elevation: 140 m.

Vegetation: Sumac, beech and maple.

Parent Material: Till, predominantly of dolomite, limestone, shale, and gneissic materials.

Soil Horizon	Depth (cm)	Description
A11	0 - 7.5	Grayish-yellow brown (10YR 5/2m, 10YR 5/2d) pebbly sandy loam; weak granular structure; firm moist consistence; slightly sticky and plastic.
A12	7.5 - 20.5	Dull yellowish-brown (10YR 5/3m), and dull yellow orange (10YR 6/3d) pebbly loam; single grain-weak granular structure; firm moist consistence; slightly sticky and plastic.
C1ox	20.5 - 34	Dull yellow orange (10YR 7/2m, 10YR 7/2d) pebbly sandy loam; massive structure; friable moist consistence; slightly sticky and plastic.
IIC2ox	34 - 61	Dull yellow orange (10YR 7/3m, 10YR 7/3d) pebbly loamy sand; massive structure; loose moist consistence; nonsticky and nonplastic.
IIICn	61+	Grayish-yellow (2.5Y 7/2m) and light yellow (5Y 7/3d) pebbly silt loam; massive structure; very friable moist consistence; slightly sticky and plastic.

Profile: R2

Age: post-Leaside

Location: Little Rouge Creek.

Elevation: 183 m.

Vegetation: Maple, beech, hemlock and cedar forest.

Parent Material: Till and loess, predominantly of dolomite, limestone, shale, granitic and gneissic materials.

Soil Horizon	Depth (cm)	Description
O1	0 - 2.5	Black (10YR 2/1m).
A1	0 - 18	Brownish-black (10YR 2/3m), to grayish-yellow brown (10YR 4/2d) loam; granular structure; firm moist consistence; sticky and plastic; tubular pores and root channels; numerous worms.
B2t	18 - 46	Dull-yellowish brown (10YR 5/4m, 10YR 5/4d) loam; weak blocky structure; firm moist consistence; sticky and plastic; tubular pores and root channels; few worms present.
IICox	46 - 89	Mottled dull yellowish-brown (10YR 5/4m), dark brown (10YR 3/3m), and dull yellow orange (10YR 6/4d) clay; blocky structure; very firm moist consistence; sticky and plastic; few worms and worm casts present.
IICn	89+	Grayish-yellow (2.5Y 6/2m, 2.5Y 7/2d) pebbly loam; massive structure; firm moist consistence; sticky and plastic.

34

Profile: R7

Age: post-Leaside

Location: 260 m north of Steeles Avenue, 200 m west of Petticoat Creek.

Elevation: 187 m.

Vegetation: Mixed-hardwood forest consisting of beech, maple and hemlock.

Parent Material: Till and loess, predominantly of dolomite, shale and granitic materials.

Soil Horizon	Depth (cm)	Description
O1	0 – 6	Black (10YR 1/1m).
A1	0 – 15	Black (10YR 2/1m), brownish-gray (10YR 4/1d) loam; granular structure; friable to firm moist consistence; slightly sticky and plastic; fibrous root systems.
B2ir	15 – 27.5	Dull yellowish brown (10YR 5/4m, 10YR 5/3d) loam; blocky structure; firm to friable moist consistence; sticky and plastic; small to medium root channels; small roots extend laterally at the base of the horizon.
IIClox	27.5 – 55.5	Dull yellowish brown (10YR 5/4m), and dull yellow orange (10YR 6/4d) loam; weak blocky to massive structure; friable moist consistence; sticky and plastic; few medium root channels through the horizon.
IIC2mox	55.5 – 104	Dull yellow orange (10YR 6/3m, and 10YR 7/2d) pebbly loam; massive structure; firm moist consistence; sticky and plastic.
IICnm	104+	Dull yellow (2.5Y 6/4m) to grayish yellow (2.5Y 7/2d) pebbly loam; massive structure; firm to very friable moist consistence; very sticky and plastic.

Profile: R6

Age: post-Leaside

Location: 290 m north of Steeles Avenue, 200 m west of Petticoat Creek.

Elevation: 187 m.

Vegetation: forest ecotone; grasses, maple, beech, hemlock.

Parent Material: Till and loess, predominantly of dolomite, shale, granitic and gneissic materials.

Soil Horizon	Depth (cm)	Description
O1	0 – 3	Black (10YR 2/1m).
A1	0 – 18	Brownish-black (10YR 3/2m), grayish-yellow brown (10YR 4/2d) loam; granular structure; firm moist consistence; sticky and plastic; fine to medium roots.
A2	18 – 30.5	Dull yellowish-brown (10YR 5/3m), dull yellow orange (10YR 6/3d) pebbly loam; weak granular structure; firm moist consistence; sticky and plastic; fine to medium roots.
B2j	30.5 – 68.5	Brown (10YR 4/4m), dull yellowish-brown (10YR 5/4d) clay loam; weak blocky structure; firm moist consistence; very sticky and plastic; root channels penetrate the horizon.
IICmox	68.5 – 106.5	Brown (10YR 4/4m), dull yellow orange (10YR 7/3d) pebbly loam; massive structure; firm moist consistence; sticky and plastic; undulatory lower boundary.
IICn(1)	106.5+	Yellowish-brown (2.5Y 5/4m), light yellow (2.5Y 7/3d) pebbly loam; massive structure; firm to very firm moist consistence; very sticky and plastic; sample collected at 127 cm.
IICn(2)		Yellowish-brown (2.5Y 5/4m), light yellow (2.5Y 7/3d) pebbly loam; massive structure; firm to very firm moist consistence; very sticky and plastic; sample collected at 178.5 cm depth.

Table 2.1 Continued Next Page

Table 2.1 Continued. Relict soil profiles[ab] from stands of mixed-hardwood forest.

Profile: R8

Age: post-Leaside

Location: Stream cut, Rouge River, 400 m north of Sheppard Avenue.

Elevation: 91 m.

Vegetation: Maple, beech and hemlock.

Parent Material: Till predominantly of dolomite, limestone, shale, granitic and gneissic materials.

Soil Horizon	Depth (cm)	Description
O1	0 - 3	Black (10YR 1/1m).
A11	0 - 7.5	Black (10YR 2/1m) and brownish-gray (10YR 4/1d) loam; granular structure; firm moist consistence; slightly sticky and plastic; numerous small and medium root systems; numerous worms.
A12	7.5 - 17.5	Brown (10YR 4/4m) and grayish-yellow brown (10YR 5/2d) loam; granular structure; firm moist consistence; slightly sticky and plastic; numerous small and medium root systems; numerous worms and worm casts.
B21r	17.5 - 35.5	Dark brown (10YR 3/4), and dull yellow orange (10YR 6/3d) loam; blocky structure; firm moist consistence; very sticky and plastic; frequent weathered gneissic cobbles and pebbles; root systems penetrate the horizon.
C1ox	35.5 - 50.5	Brown (10YR 4/6m) and dull yellow orange (10YR 7/2d) silty clay loam; massive structure; firm moist consistence; sticky and plastic.
C2ox	50.5 - 96	Brown (10YR 4/6m) and dull yellow orange (10YR 7/3d) pebbly silt loam; massive structure; firm moist consistence; sticky and plastic.

Profile: R10

Age: post-Leaside

Location: Stream cut, Rouge River, 60 m north of Finch Avenue.

Elevation: 122 m.

Vegetation: Beech, maple and hemlock.

Parent Material: Till and loess, predominantly of dolomite, limestone, shale, granitic and gneissic materials.

Soil Horizon	Depth (cm)	Description
O1	0 - 3.5	Brownish-black (10YR 2/2).
A11	0 - 7.5	Brownish-black (10YR 2/3m) and brownish-gray (10YR 4/1d) loam; granular structure; friable moist consistence; slightly sticky and plastic; numerous fine and medium roots; few worms and wormholes.
A12	7.5 - 15.0	Dull yellowish-brown (10YR 5/3m) and dull yellow orange (10YR 6/3d) pebbly loam; weak granular structure; firm moist consistence; sticky and plastic; numerous fine and medium roots; numerous worms.
IIB2t	15 - 40.5	Mottled brown (10YR 4/6m), light yellow (2.5Y 7/4m) and dull yellow orange (10YR 6/4d) pebbly clay loam; weak blocky structure; firm to very firm moist consistence; very sticky and plastic; numerous fine and medium roots; numerous worms and wormholes.
IICox	40.5 - 114	Dull yellow orange (10YR 6/3m) and grayish yellow (2.5Y 7/2d) pebbly loam; weak blocky structure; firm moist consistence; sticky and plastic.
IICn	114+	Dull yellow (2.5Y 6/3m) and grayish-yellow (2.5Y 7/2d) pebbly loam; weak blocky to massive structure; firm moist consistence; slightly sticky and plastic.

Cn(1) 96+ — Olive yellow (10Y 6/3m) and light yellow (2.5Y 7/3d) pebbly loam; massive structure; very firm moist consistence; very sticky and very plastic. Sample collected at 178.5 cm depth.

Cn(2) — Grayish yellow (2.5Y 6/2m) and light yellow (2.5Y 7/3d) pebbly loam; massive structure; very firm moist consistence; very sticky and very plastic. Sample collected at 239 cm depth.

Profile: WD2

Age: post-Leaside

Location: Stream cut, west Duffin Creek, Clarkes Hollow.

Elevation: 165 m.

Vegetation: grass.

Parent Material: Till, beech, and eolian sediment, predominantly of dolomite, limestone, shale and gneissic materials.

Soil Horizon	Depth (cm)	Description
01	0 - 4	Black (10YR 2/1m).
A1	0 - 20	Brownish-black (10YR 2/3m) and brownish-gray (10YR 4/1d) sandy loam; granular structure; friable moist consistence; slightly sticky and plastic; numerous small, medium and large (>10 mm) roots.
Bir	20 - 27.5	Brown (10YR 4/6m) and dull yellow orange (10YR 6/4d) sandy loam; weak blocky structure; friable moist consistence; sticky and slightly plastic; numerous small, medium and large (>10 mm) roots.
Clox	27.5 - 68	Dull yellow orange (10YR 7/4m, 10YR 6/3d) loamy sand; massive structure; friable moist consistence; sticky and nonplastic; numerous medium and large roots.
IIC2ox	68 - 80.5	Dull reddish-brown (5YR 4/4m) and brown (7.5YR 4/4d) sandy loam; massive structure; firm moist consistence; sticky and slightly plastic.
IIIC3ox	80.5 - 106	Light yellow (2.5Y 7/3m) and dull yellow orange (10YR 7/3d) silty clay loam; weak blocky structure; firm moist consistence; very sticky and plastic.
IVCn	106+	Light yellow (2.5Y 7/3m, 2.5Y 7/3d) pebbly clay loam; massive structure; firm moist consistence; very sticky and plastic.

---

a Terms and horizon nomenclature employed are in standard use with the U.S.D.A. (1951, 1960). Soil colors are given as moist (m) and dry (d).

b Soil pit locations (e.g. L1, R7) can be located on Figs. 3, 4, 5 and 6.

Table 2.2. Particle-size distribution[a] for material >2mm of the horizons in
Table 2.1. The data are given in weight-percentage of dry mineral
matter and bulk weight-percentage of sand, silt and clay (< 2mm).

Sample[b]	Depth (cm)	Pebble Very Large 64-32 mm (-6/-5μ)	Pebble Large 32-16 mm (-5/-4μ)	Pebble Medium 16-8 mm (-4/-3μ)	Pebble Small 8-4 mm (-3/-2μ)	Granule 4-2 mm (-2/-1μ)	Total Sample Pebble %	Total Sample Granule %	Total Sample Sand-Silt-Clay %	<2mm Fractions Sand %	<2mm Fractions Silt %	<2mm Fractions Clay %
Site Horizon												
L1-A11	0-7.5	...	...	1.6	1.2	3.3	2.8	3.3	93.9	54.8	38.7	6.5
L1-A12	7.5-20.5	...	2.2	4.0	2.3	6.7	8.5	6.7	84.7	51.7	38.8	9.5
L1-Clox	20.5-34	...	...	...	0.1	0.2	0.1	0.2	99.7	48.3	45.7	6.0
L1-C2ox	34 -61	...	...	...	...	0.3		0.3	99.7	86.6	9.4	4.0
L1-Cn	61+	...	...	1.1	2.4	0.8	3.5	0.8	93.0	38.0	53.5	8.5
R2-A1	0-18	...	...	...	0.5	0.4	0.5	0.4	99.1	47.3	39.7	13.0
R2-B2t	18-46	...	0.6	1.1	0.4	0.7	2.1	0.7	97.2	43.8	35.7	20.5
R2-Cox	46-89	...	1.9	1.2	0.8	1.2	3.9	1.2	94.9	30.0	27.0	43.0
R2-Cn	89+	...	3.1	3.2	2.9	3.0	9.2	3.0	87.8	47.6	32.4	20.0
R6-A1	0-18	...	...	0.1	0.3	0.2	0.4	0.2	99.4	42.4	45.6	12.0
R6-A2	18-30.5	...	...	...	0.4	0.6	0.4	0.6	99.0	40.1	38.9	21.0
R6-B2t	30.5-68.5	...	0.3	1.3	1.1	0.9	2.7	0.9	96.4	39.0	34.0	27.0
R6-Cmox	68.5-106.5	...	2.9	3.6	3.4	2.6	10.0	2.6	87.4	42.4	34.6	23.0
R6-Cn(1)	125	8.2	5.4	3.7	3.1	2.5	20.4	2.5	77.1	43.0	34.0	23.0
R6-Cn(2)	178.5	...	4.0	3.5	2.8	2.5	10.3	2.5	87.2	43.3	33.7	23.0
R7-A1	0-15	...	...	0.2	0.2	0.1	0.4	0.1	99.5	44.0	46.0	10.0
R7-B2ir	15-27.5	...	0.2	0.3	0.4	0.4	0.9	0.4	98.7	36.4	43.6	20.0
R7-Clox	27.5-55.5	...	0.3	0.1	0.4	0.5	0.8	0.5	98.7	38.1	34.9	27.0
R7-C2mox	55.5-104	10.2	1.3	2.8	2.3	2.9	16.6	2.9	80.5	42.5	31.5	26.0
R7-Cnm	104+	...	6.2	2.4	3.2	2.5	11.8	2.5	85.7	40.9	35.1	24.0

R8-A11	0-7.5	...	1.0	0.8	1.2	0.8	3.0	0.8	96.2	42.8	39.8	17.4
R8-A12	7.5-17.5	...	3.8	0.7	1.1	0.7	5.6	0.7	93.7	46.9	36.4	16.7
R8-B2ir	17.5-35.5	5.2	0.6	0.8	1.1	1.3	7.7	1.3	91.0	33.9	47.8	18.3
R8-C1ox	35.5-50.5	...	...	...	0.1	0.3	0.1	0.3	99.6	9.8	63.0	27.2
R8-C2ox	50.5-96	...	3.2	0.4	1.7	0.7	5.3	0.7	94.0	14.1	62.1	23.8
R8-Cn(1)	178.5	...	1.8	2.7	3.3	2.7	7.8	2.7	89.5	49.0	37.0	14.0
R8-Cn(2)	239	...	2.1	2.1	2.8	3.1	7.0	3.1	89.9	47.8	39.3	12.9
R10-A11	0-7.5	...	0.4	0.6	0.4	0.9	1.4	0.9	97.7	36.2	47.4	16.4
R10-A12	7.5-15	...	...	0.5	0.4	1.2	0.9	1.2	97.9	35.6	43.9	20.5
R10-B2t	15-40.5	...	3.1	3.5	2.4	1.5	9.0	1.5	89.5	38.4	30.6	31.0
R10-Cox	40.5-114	1.8	5.5	4.3	2.6	2.3	14.2	2.3	83.5	45.5	34.9	19.6
R10-Cn	114+	...	1.0	4.2	2.9	2.7	8.1	2.7	89.2	42.9	39.1	18.0
WD2-A1	0-20	...	...	...	0.1	0.1	0.1	0.1	99.8	71.6	22.4	6.0
WD2-Bir	20-27.5	...	...	...	0.2	0.4	0.2	0.4	99.4	72.7	20.3	7.0
WD2-C1ox	27.5-68	...	...	0.1	0.2	0.3	0.3	0.3	99.4	77.9	16.6	5.5
WD2-C2ox	68-80.5	...	...	...	0.1	0.1	0.1	0.1	99.8	75.1	6.4	18.5
WD2-C3ox	80.5-106	...	...	...	...	0.1	...	0.1	99.9	9.4	55.1	35.5
WD2-Cn	106+	16.6	2.9	1.8	1.5	1.5	22.8	1.5	75.7	39.9	32.1	28.0

[a]Coarse particle sizes (64 mm-63μ) determined by sieving; fine particle sizes (63-1.95μ) determined by hydrometer; ... nil.

[b]Soil pit locations (e.g. R1, WD1) can be located on Figs. 3, 4, 5 and 6.

39

horizons have a higher concentration of clay when compared
with the parent material. The clay grade-sizes show evidence
for illuviation, especially at sites R2, R6, R7, R8, R10, and
WD2. Curves showing the granulometric compositions of horizons in each profile are given in Figs. 2.8, 2.9, 2.10,
2.11, 2.12, 2.13, and 2.14. These indicate a close correlation between sites of the sand-silt-clay ratios, with minor
departures at sites L1, R10, and WD2. These departures are
explained by variations in the original parent material (e.g.
till, beach deposits, and eolian cover). The particle-size
curves also indicate the relative amount of weathering or
reduction in size which can be calculated by comparing the
Cn curve with curves for each soil horizon. Sites R2, R8,
and WD2 show the greatest degree of weathering, while sites
L1, R6, R7, and R10 show a close correspondence of the parent
material curve with curves for each soil horizon.

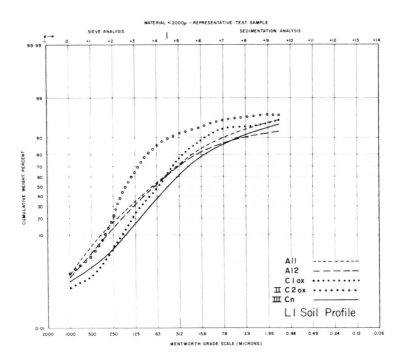

Figure 2.8. Particle-size analysis of profile L1.

40

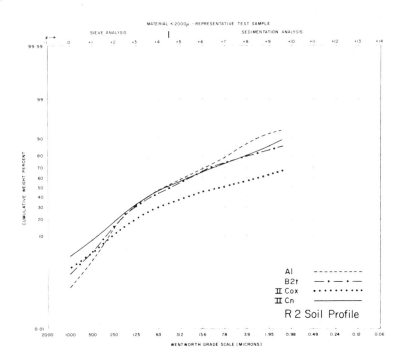

Figure 2.9. Particle-size analysis of profile R2.

41

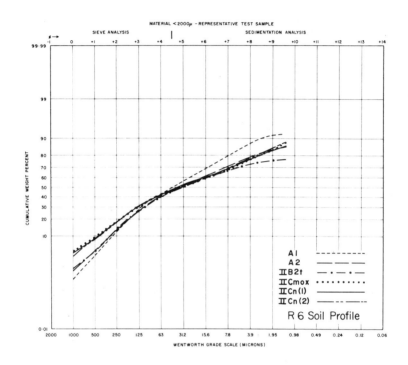

Figure 2.10. Particle-size analysis of profile R6.

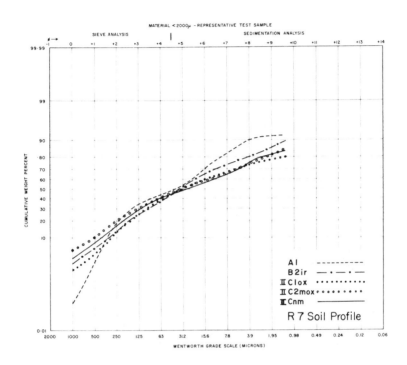

Figure 2.11. Particle-size analysis of profile R7.

43

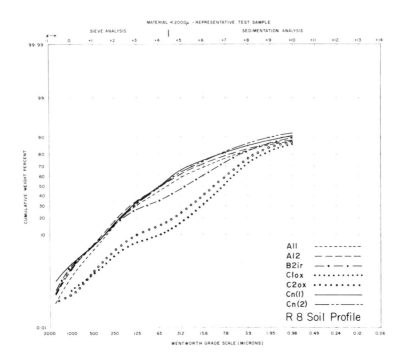

Figure 2.12.   Particle-size analysis of profile R8.

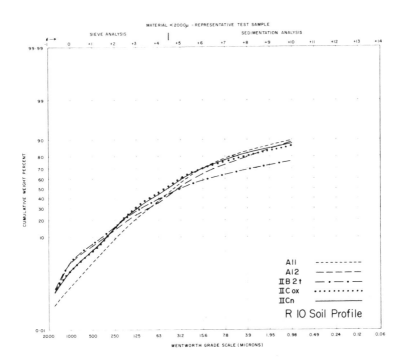

Figure 2.13. Particle-size analysis of profile R10.

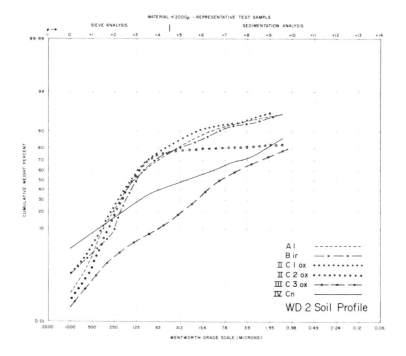

Figure 2.14. Particle-size analysis of profile WD2.

The distributions of silt and clay with depth in each profile are given in Figs. 2.15A and 2.15B. The tendency for silt to dominate in the solum (A + B horizons) suggests eolian deposition. Silt is either evenly distributed or dominated by the coarse grade-sizes (Table 2.3). Fig. 2.16 shows the particle-size distribution with samples ranging from loamy sand to clay.

Clay Mineralogy

The mineralogy of the clay grade-size (< 1.95μ) was studied by X-ray diffraction. The minerals detected are shown in Table 2.4.

46

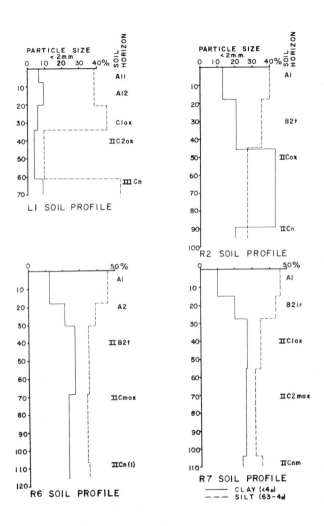

Figure 2.15A.   Particle-size distribution with depth
for soils forming on Leaside Till.   Soil
nomenclature is: Bir for color B
horizon; Bt for textural B horizon; Cox
for oxidized C horizon; and Cn for unweathered, unconsolidated and undifferentiated parent material.

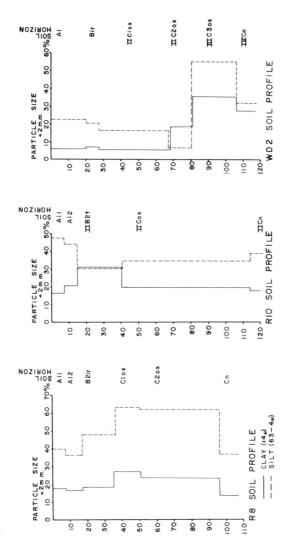

Figure 2.15B. Particle-size distribution with depth for soils forming on Leaside Till.

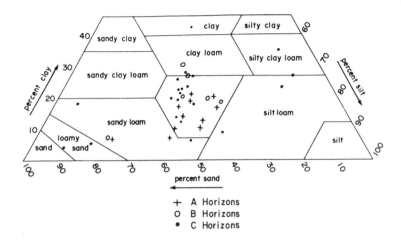

Figure 2.16.   Particle-size classification of soils
forming on glacial deposits. Textures
of relict soils vary from loamy sand
to clay. Textural classification
follows the Soil Survey Staff (1951).

Kaolinite was identified by a reflection at 7.1 Å
which is unaffected by glycolation and disappears after
heating for 2 hours at 550°C. Halloysite, a companion kaolin
mineral, is identified by an asymmetrical peak at 7.2 Å with
the steeper side of the reflection facing higher d-spacings.
001 reflections sharpen and expand to 7.5 Å after heating
at 140°C for 15 hours. Halloysite is unaffected by glycolation, and collapses after heating at 550°C for 2 hours.

Illite gives asymmetrical peaks at 10.1 Å, and usually
possesses a moderate crystalline form; peak asymmetry towards
the low angle region may reflect variations in cation inter-
layering and/or slight hydration. 001 reflections sharpen
after heating at 550°C for two hours. Montmorillonite produces reflections between 12.5 and 14.5 Å which expand to
17.0 Å after saturation with ethylene glycol (15 hours at
65°C). Mixed-layer illite-montmorillonite, randomly inter-
stratified, produces reflections very close to the dominant
layer (e.g. illite) in the region between 10.1 and 12.5 Å.

Table 2.3. Particle-size distribution[a] for material <2mm of the horizons in Table 2.1. The data are given in weight-percentage and cumulative weight-percent of dry mineral matter.

Sample[b]	Depth (cm)	SAND					SILT				CLAY	
		Very Coarse 2-1 mm (-1/0Ø)	Coarse 1mm-500µ (0-1Ø)	Medium 500-250µ (1-2Ø)	Fine 250-125µ (2-3Ø)	Very Fine 125-63µ (3-4Ø)	Coarse 63-31.2µ (4-5Ø)	Medium 31.2-15.6µ (5-6Ø)	Fine 15.6-7.8µ (6-7Ø)	Very Fine 7.8-3.9µ (7-8Ø)	Coarse 3.9-1.95µ (8-9Ø)	Fine <1.95µ (>9Ø)
Site Horizon												
L1-A11	0-7.5	1.06	4.62	10.62	17.92	20.60	16.68	13.0	5.5	3.5	1.7	4.8
		1.06	5.68	16.30	34.22	54.82	71.50	84.5	90.0	93.5	95.2	100
L1-A12	7.5-20.5	0.84	3.08	10.10	17.58	20.12	19.28	9.5	7.0	3.0	1.5	8.0
		0.84	3.92	14.02	31.60	51.72	71.0	80.5	87.5	90.5	92.0	100
L1-C1ox	20.5-34	.34	.52	4.94	18.22	24.24	27.74	12.5	4.8	.7	1.0	5.0
		.34	.86	5.80	24.02	48.26	76.0	88.5	93.3	94.0	95.0	100
L1-C2ox	34-61	1.14	2.52	17.38	43.52	22.06	4.88	2.5	2.0	.7	.3	3.0
		1.14	3.66	21.04	64.56	86.62	91.5	94.0	96.0	96.7	97.0	100
L1-Cn	61+	.62	1.00	3.48	11.94	20.96	24.0	16.0	8.5	4.5	4.0	5.0
		.62	1.62	5.10	17.04	38.00	62.0	78.0	86.5	91.0	95.0	100
R2-A1	0-18	.42	2.54	12.26	18.64	13.46	11.68	9.0	10.0	9.0	5.0	8.0
		.42	2.96	15.22	33.86	47.32	59.0	68.0	78.0	87.0	92.0	100
R2-B2t	18-46	1.02	3.34	10.90	15.90	12.66	10.68	11.5	8.0	5.5	4.5	16.00
		1.02	4.36	15.26	31.16	43.82	54.5	66.0	74.0	79.5	84.0	100
R2-Cox	46-89	1.60	2.64	6.60	10.00	9.18	7.98	7.5	4.5	7.0	6.5	36.5
		1.60	4.24	10.84	20.84	30.02	38.0	45.5	50.0	57.0	63.5	100
R2-Cn	89+	3.86	4.94	10.32	15.16	13.30	8.42	10.0	7.0	7.0	6.0	14.0
		3.86	8.80	19.12	34.28	47.58	56.0	66.0	73.0	80.0	86.0	100
R6-A1	0-18	.80	2.92	9.22	15.74	13.72	13.60	13.0	10.0	9.0	3.5	8.5
		.80	3.72	12.94	28.68	42.40	56.0	69.0	79.0	88.0	91.5	100
R6-A2	18-30.5	1.42	3.30	8.64	13.84	12.90	11.90	9.5	8.5	9.0	5.0	16.0
		1.42	4.72	13.36	27.20	40.10	52.0	61.5	70.0	79.0	84.0	100
R6-B2t	30.5-68.5	1.62	3.14	8.54	13.52	12.22	10.96	9.0	7.0	7.0	3.0	24.0
		1.62	4.76	13.30	26.82	39.04	50.0	59.0	66.0	73.0	76.0	100
R6-Cmox	68.5-106.5	4.48	5.20	9.06	12.58	11.06	8.62	8.0	8.0	10.0	7.0	16.0
		4.48	9.68	18.74	31.32	42.38	51.0	59.0	67.0	77.0	84.0	100.0
R6-Cn(1)	125	4.48	5.00	9.14	12.80	11.60	9.98	7.0	9.0	8.0	6.0	17.0
		4.48	9.48	18.62	31.42	43.02	53.0	60.0	69.0	77.0	83.0	100.0
R6-Cn(2)	178.5	3.44	5.12	9.60	13.26	11.90	8.68	8.0	9.0	8.0	7.5	15.5
		3.44	8.56	18.16	31.42	43.32	52.0	60.0	69.0	77.0	84.5	100

Sample	Depth											
R7-A1	0-15	0.14	2.64	15.82	15.56	9.88	8.96	17.0	11.5	8.5	1.5	8.5
		0.14	2.78	18.60	34.16	44.04	53.0	70.0	81.5	90.0	91.5	100
R7-B2ir	15-27.5	2.50	3.42	7.92	11.52	11.00	15.64	13.0	8.5	6.5	6.0	14.0
		2.50	5.92	13.84	25.36	36.36	52.0	65.0	73.5	80.0	86.0	100
R7-Clox	27.5-55.5	1.68	3.12	8.24	13.12	11.98	11.86	10.0	7.0	7.0	5.0	22.0
		1.68	4.80	13.04	26.16	38.14	50.0	60.0	67.0	73.0	78.0	100
R7-C2mox	55.5-104	5.40	5.36	9.28	11.92	10.52	8.52	7.0	8.0	8.0	7.5	18.5
		5.40	10.76	20.04	31.96	42.48	51.0	58.0	66.0	74.0	81.5	100
R7-Cnm	104+	3.34	4.70	9.22	12.66	10.94	7.64	7.5	8.5	11.5	6.0	18.0
		3.34	8.04	17.26	29.92	40.86	48.5	56.0	64.5	76.0	82.0	100
R8-A11	0-7.5	0.8	3.5	11.1	15.2	12.3	15.5	10.0	8.4	5.8	3.6	13.8
		0.8	4.3	15.4	30.5	42.8	58.3	68.3	76.7	82.6	86.2	100
R8-A12	7.5-17.5	1.4	4.4	12.6	16.6	11.9	15.6	8.9	7.0	4.9	3.2	13.5
		1.4	5.8	18.4	34.9	46.9	62.5	71.4	78.4	83.3	86.5	100
R8-B2ir	17.5-35.5	1.8	3.9	10.2	10.8	7.2	12.6	13.9	12.7	8.8	4.8	13.4
		1.8	5.7	15.9	26.7	33.9	46.4	60.3	73.0	81.7	86.6	100
R8-Clox	35.5-50.5	0.3	0.8	2.5	3.6	2.7	7.8	15.0	21.3	18.9	9.6	17.6
		0.3	1.0	3.5	7.1	9.8	17.5	32.6	53.9	72.8	82.3	100
R8-C2ox	50.5-96	0.2	1.0	3.4	5.3	4.2	9.7	16.3	19.5	16.6	8.1	15.7
		0.2	1.2	4.6	9.9	14.1	23.8	40.2	59.7	76.2	84.3	100
R8-Cn(1)	178.5	2.0	3.7	10.7	17.8	14.8	18.0	8.2	6.4	4.4	2.9	11.1
		2.0	5.7	16.5	34.2	49.0	67.0	75.2	81.6	86.0	88.9	100
R8-Cn(2)	239	1.5	3.8	10.3	17.1	15.1	16.6	9.7	7.7	5.2	3.1	9.8
		1.5	5.3	15.6	32.7	47.0	64.5	74.2	81.9	87.1	90.2	100
R10-A11	0-7.5	0.5	2.1	6.4	12.6	14.6	20.2	13.8	7.8	5.5	3.6	12.9
		0.5	2.6	9.0	21.6	36.2	56.4	70.2	78.1	83.6	87.1	100
R10-A12	7.5-15	2.7	3.6	7.4	11.2	10.7	16.7	13.0	8.0	6.3	5.2	15.3
		2.7	6.4	13.8	24.9	35.6	52.3	65.3	73.3	79.5	84.7	100
R10-B2t	15-40.5	2.7	4.3	8.7	12.9	9.8	11.8	7.9	5.7	5.1	4.1	26.9
		2.7	7.0	15.7	28.6	38.4	50.3	58.2	63.9	69.0	73.1	100
R10-Cox	40.5-114	1.6	3.2	10.4	16.8	13.6	15.6	8.6	6.2	4.5	3.6	16.0
		1.6	4.8	15.2	31.9	45.5	61.1	69.6	75.9	80.4	83.9	100
R10-Cn	114+	1.6	3.2	9.7	15.7	12.7	16.7	10.2	7.4	4.8	3.8	14.2
		1.6	4.8	14.5	30.2	42.9	59.6	69.8	77.2	82.0	85.8	100

Table 2.3 Continued Next Page

Table 2.3 Continued. Particle-size distribution[a] for material <2mm of the horizons in Table 2.1. The data are given in weight-percentage and cumulative weight-percent of dry mineral matter.

Sample[b]	Depth (cm)	SAND					SILT				CLAY	
		Very Coarse 2-1 mm (-1/0∅)	Coarse 1mm-500μ (0-1∅)	Medium 500-250μ (1-2∅)	Fine 250-125μ (2-3∅)	Very Fine 125-63μ (3-4∅)	Coarse 63-31.2μ (4-5∅)	Medium 31.2-15.6μ (5-6∅)	Fine 15.6-7.8μ (6-7∅)	Very Fine 7.8-3.9μ (7-8∅)	Coarse 2.9-1.95μ (8-9∅)	Fine <1.95μ (79∅)
WD2-A1	0-20	0.16	2.22	19.12	31.54	18.60	9.86	7.0	3.5	2.0	1.3	4.7
		0.16	2.38	21.50	53.04	71.64	81.5	88.5	92.0	94.0	95.3	100
WD2-Bir	20-27.5	0.64	2.26	16.36	33.22	20.22	7.8	5.0	6.0	1.5	2.0	5.0
		0.64	2.90	19.26	52.48	72.70	80.5	85.5	91.5	93.0	95.0	100
WD2-Clox	27.5-68	0.60	3.46	21.20	33.60	19.02	8.12	5.0	2.0	1.5	1.5	4.0
		0.60	4.06	25.26	58.86	77.88	86.0	91.0	93.0	94.5	96.0	100
WD2-C2ox	68-80.5	0.08	1.26	16.44	37.26	20.04	2.92	2.0	0.5	0.5	1.0	17.5
		0.08	1.34	17.78	55.04	75.08	78.0	80.0	81.0	81.5	82.5	100
WD2-C3ox	80.5-106	0.04	0.42	1.72	3.46	3.76	10.6	16.0	17.0	12.0	9.0	26.0
		0.04	0.46	2.18	5.64	9.40	20.0	36.0	53.0	65.0	74.0	100
WD2-Cn	106+	3.74	4.38	8.40	12.02	11.32	8.14	8.0	10.0	6.0	10.0	18.0
		3.74	8.12	16.52	28.54	39.86	48.0	56.0	66.0	72.0	82.0	100

[a] Coarse particle-sizes (2 mm – 63μ) determined by sieving; fine particle-sizes (63-1.95μ) determined by hydrometer.

[b] Soil pits (e.g. L1, R2) can be located on Figs. 3, 4, 5 and 6.

Chlorite yields air-dried reflections (001) at 13.8 to 14.2 Å
which remain unaffected by glycolation, and heating at 500°C
for two hours. 002 peaks at 7 Å and 004 reflections at 3.5 Å
disappear or undergo partial collapse after heating at 500°C
for two hours. Some samples produce the same relative intensity of 001 and 002 reflections suggesting the presence
of the dioctahedral form of chlorite (Aℓ), while others give
smaller 001 reflections indicating the presence of triocta-
hedral chlorite (Fe + Mg).

Quartz gives reflections at 3.35 Å, feldspar at 3.18 Å,
and calcite at 3.01 Å (Brown, 1972).

The variance in mineral content of the <2ν grade-size
from horizon to horizon (Table 2.4) reflects the degree of
weathering and leaching in each profile. The data indicate
that clay minerals are present in the upper till bodies, and
throughout the soil profiles. The relative abundance of
each mineral in each soil profile is given in Table 2.4.

Mixed-layer illite-montmorillonite is the most abundant
clay mineral within the 2:1 and 2:1:1 clay mineral suites.
There is an overall tendency for this clay mineral to increase
with depth in the soils, while the inverse relationship pre-
vails in the case of chlorite, halloysite, kaolinite, and
illite. This trend suggests that some chlorite, kaolinite,
and halloysite form from the weathering of mixed-layer illite-
montmorillonite. The small amount of montmorillonite in most
soil profiles is attributed to the humid climate and overall
leaching processes which remove Si^{+4} and some Na^+ and Ca^{+2}.
Minor amounts of this clay mineral are found in the subsurface
horizons of sites R2 and WD2. The data suggest that several
1:1, 2:1, and 2:1:1 clay minerals owe their origin to re-
crystallization of mixed layer clays which involves a complete
chemical change in the composition of the original mineral.
The relatively small amount of kaolin minerals in most profiles is attributed to the overall small percentage ($\sim$20
percent) of feldspar-bearing rocks in most soil profiles
(kaolinite is pseudomorphous after feldspar), and to pH's
which are neutral to moderately alkaline.

Quartz and feldspar (<2ν) are evenly distributed
throughout the profiles, whereas calcite is generally present
only in the lower C horizons and in the parent material.
The subsurface horizons at sites R6 and R7 are both cemented,
and here calcite is abundant owing to the slow rate of car-
bonation as a result of slow water infiltration rates.

Table 2.4. X-ray analyses of the clay fraction (< 2μ) of the horizons in Table 2.1.

Sample[b]	Depth (cm)	Mineralogy[a]								
		Chlorite	Halloysite	Illite	Kaolinite	Montmorillonite	Mixed-Layer Illite-Montmorillonite	Feldspar	Quartz	Calcite
Site Horizon										
L1-A11	0-7.5			tr	tr		xx	tr	xx	
L1-A12	7.5-20.5						xx	tr	x	
L1-C1	20.5-34						xxx	x	xxx	
L1-C2	34-61						xx	x	xxx	
L1-Cn	61+			tr			xxx	tr	x	
R2-A1	0-18	x		tr	tr		tr		x	
R2-B2t	18-46	xx	tr	tr	x		tr	tr	xxx	
R2-Cox	46-89	x	tr	xxx	x	tr	xx	tr	xxx	
R2-Cn	89+			tr			x	tr	x	xxx
R6-A1	0-18	tr		tr	tr		tr	tr	x	
R6-A2	18-30.5	x	tr	x	tr		x	x	xxx	
R6-B2t	30.5-68.5	x	tr	xx	tr		xx	tr	xx	
R6-Cmox	68.5-106.5	tr		x	tr		xx	tr	x	xxx
R6-Cn(1)	127	tr		x	tr		xxx	tr	x	xx
R6-Cn(2)	178.5	tr		x	tr		xx	tr	xx	xx
R7-A1	0-15	tr					tr	tr	x	tr
R7-B2ir	15-27.5	x	tr	tr	tr		tr		xx	
R7-Clox	27.5-55.5	x	tr	x	tr		x	tr	xx	
R7-C2mox	55.5-104			tr			xxx	tr	tr	xxx
R7-Cnm	104+			tr			xxx	tr	x	xxx
R8-A11	0-7.5	tr	tr	tr	tr			tr	xxx	
R8-A12	7.5-17.5	tr	tr	tr	tr		tr	tr	xxx	
R8-B2ir	17.5-35.5	tr	tr	x	tr		tr	tr	xxx	
R8-Clox	35.5-50.5	tr		tr	tr		tr	tr	xxx	
R8-C2ox	50.5-96	tr		x	tr		tr	tr	xxx	
R8-Cn(1)	178.5	tr		x	tr		tr	tr	xxx	
R8-Cn(2)	239	tr		x	tr		tr	x	xxx	

Sample[b]	Depth (cm)								
R10-A11	0–7.5	tr	...	...	...	tr	tr	xxx	...
R10-A12	7.5–15	tr	tr	tr	...	tr	tr	xxx	...
R10-B2t	15–40.5	tr	tr?	tr	...	tr	tr	xxx	...
R10-Cox	40.5–114	...	...	tr	...	x	x	xxx	...
R10-Cn	114+	...	...	tr	...	x	x	xxx	tr
WD2-A1	0–20	x	...	tr	...	xxx	tr	xxx	...
WD2-Bir	20–27.5	xx	tr	tr	...	...	tr	xxx	...
WD2-C1ox	27.5–68	x	tr	tr	...	...	tr	xxx	...
WD2-C2ox	68–80.5	x	tr	tr	tr	tr	tr	xx	...
WD2-C3ox	80.5–106	tr	tr	tr	tr	xx	tr	xx	xx
WD2-Cn	106+	tr	...	tr	tr	x	tr	x	xxx

[a]Mineral abundance is based on peak height: minor amount (tr); small amount (x); medium amount (xx); abundant (xxx); ... no detection.

[b]Soil pits (e.g. L1, R2) can be located on Figs. 3, 4, 5 and 6.

55

Soil Chemistry

The soil pH ranges from neutral to strongly alkaline, and generally increases with depth in the profiles (Table 2.5). This trend is paralleled by the general tendency for exchangeable H^+ (meq./100 g) activity to decrease with depth in the profiles. Exchangeable H^+ ion activity correlates closely with the presence of kaolin minerals (Table 2.4) which are found mainly in the solum.

Cation exchange capacity is highest in the solum with values ranging between 10.4 and 23.8 (meq./100 g). Total CEC is not favorable for the production of 2:1 clays like montmorillonite, and 2:1:1 clays like chlorite, but it is sufficient for 1:1 kaolin minerals and 2:1 clays like illite. The distribution of the exchangeable basic cations Ca^{+2} and Na^+, most mobile of all the basic cations, is necessary to maintain montmorillonite; K^+ and Mg^{+2} ions, less mobile than Ca^{+2} and Na^+, occur in exchange with illite and chlorite respectively. Higher amounts of Na^+, Ca^{+2}, K^+ and Mg^{+2} in some surface horizons may reflect base cycling by plants. H^+ ions are the chief exchange ions for kaolin minerals. As indicated by the tendency of Ca^{+2} and $CaCO_3$ to increase with depth, leaching processes are sufficient to remove carbonate into the subsoil. The high base saturation indicates that weathering processes are sufficient to release free ions in the solum, and leaching is only moderate at best. The data suggest that leaching processes are not sufficient to remove the mobile cations of Ca^{+2} and Na^+, or to lower the pH appreciably and move H^+ ions to depth in the profiles. The moderate to weak leaching effects are further substantiated by the tendency for salts to increase toward the surface of some profiles.

Surface soil horizons show an increase in water retention over the lower horizons as a function of high organic matter and clay-silt accumulation. The percentage of water on a dry-weight basis ranges from 0.04 to 2.40 percent.

Free iron oxide analyses indicate that Fe_2O_3 reaches 2.1 percent in the A and B horizons of most soils. These figures are comparable to soils of similar age in the Rocky Mountains (Mahaney and Fahey, 1976). The higher quantities of Fe_2O_3 are in horizons with lower pH, higher H^+ ion activity, and a higher oxidizing potential.

Organic matter, organic carbon, nitrogen, and the ratio of carbon to nitrogen tend to decrease with depth in

the profiles as a function of distance from the zone of maximum biological activity. The data indicate the magnitude
of leaching in the profiles as organic matter and organic
carbon do not leach as quickly in the cemented profiles.

Pesticides

The chemistry and structure of DDT and related organochlorides have been reviewed by Haller et al. (1945), Metcalf
(1955), and more recently by Barthel et al. (1966) and Kaufman (1966). DDT is a white colored noncrystalline powder
produced by reacting chloral with chlorobenzene in the presence of H_2SO_4, oleum, or chlorosulfuric acid as shown in
the following equation:

$$\text{(1)}$$

Pure DDT, consisting of at least 14 compounds, is made up
principally of p,p'-DDT, 2,2-bis-(p-chlorophenyl)-1,1,1-
trichloroethane, and 2-(o-chlorophenyl)-2-(p-chlorophenyl)-
1,1,1-trichlorethane (o,p'-DDT). These two compounds con-
stitute $\sim$80 percent of technical DDT, the remaining 20 percent consisting of small (<2.0 percent) to trace amounts
of DDD, tri-chloroethanol, sulfone, chlorophenylacetamide,
chlorobenzene, dichlorobenzene, and tetrachloroethane (Metcalf, 1955).

In contact with an alkali, DDT is dehydrochlorinated
by loss of hydrogen chloride to form dehydrochloro-DDT that
is oxidized to p,p'-dichlorobenzophenone as shown in Equation
2:

$$\text{(2)}$$

Table 2.5. Selected chemical properties of the <2mm fractions of the horizons in Table 2.1.

Sample[a]	Depth (cm)	pH	H+	K+	Ca++	Mg++	Na+	CEC meq/100g	CaCO3 %	CO3 %	Base Sat. %	Salts mmhos/cm	O.M. %	O.C. %	N %	C:N	P ppm 1:20 NaH CO3	Fe2O3 %	Oven Dried Moisture %
Site Horizon																			
L1-A11	0-7.5	7.5	3.92	0.18	31.5	0.84	0.31	18.41	1.06	---	100	0.66	7.67	4.45	0.24	18:1	---	1.26	0.94
L1-A12	7.5-20.5	7.7	3.32	0.12	15.4	0.28	0.20	10.46	0.12	---	100	0.51	1.94	1.13	0.06	19:1	---	2.11	1.13
L1-C1ox	20.5-34	8.3	1.81	0.19	44.2	1.0	0.22	13.58	9.19	---	100	0.48	0.86	0.50	0.04	13:1	---	1.79	0.06
L1-C2ox	34-61	8.5	tr	0.11	41.6	0.71	0.25	5.73	16.5	---	100	0.61	0.03	0.02	0.01	2:1	---	0.98	0.04
L1-Cn	61+	8.3	tr	0.11	41.6	0.84	0.22	2.52	16.8	---	100	0.60	0.05	0.03	0.01	3:1	---	0.82	0.16
R2-A1	0-18	7.2	6.8	0.16	17.9	0.82	0.02	18.76	0.07	---	100	0.45	6.60	3.83	0.26	15:1	6.37	1.23	1.92
R2-B2t	18-46	7.1	5.7	0.07	6.8	0.20	0.04	6.89	0.1	---	100	0.21	1.42	0.82	0.05	16:1	5.10	1.47	1.15
R2-Cox	46-89	7.9	4.3	0.24	25.0	0.76	0.04	14.87	0.5	---	100	0.38	1.02	0.59	0.05	12:1	2.78	1.70	2.19
R2-Cn	89+	8.4	0.8	0.11	38.0	0.53	0.09	3.56	26.6	---	100	0.41	0.23	0.13	0.01	13:1	2.12	0.75	0.38
R6-A1	0-18	7.7	4.4	0.12	12.5	0.46	tr	14.73	0.02	---	89	0.37	5.35	3.10	0.20	16:1	5.39	1.16	1.56
R6-A2	18-30.5	7.3	3.9	0.09	8.4	0.20	tr	7.41	0.03	---	100	0.23	1.08	0.63	0.05	13:1	5.55	1.12	1.03
R6-B2t	30.5-68.5	8.1	2.9	0.16	29.0	0.43	0.02	9.98	1.7	---	100	0.31	0.91	0.53	0.04	13:1	7.20	1.70	1.44
R6-Cmox	68.5-106.5	8.5	0.5	0.09	37.0	0.46	0.02	3.52	17.0	---	100	0.24	0.40	0.23	0.02	12:1	1.96	0.78	0.62
R6-Cn(1)	127	8.3	0.8	0.09	37.0	0.43	0.04	3.75	17.4	---	100	0.34	0.34	0.20	0.01	20:1	1.47	0.81	0.66
R6-Cn(2)	178.5	8.3	0.6	0.09	37.0	0.59	0.10	3.99	17.6	---	100	0.85	0.34	0.20	0.01	20:1	2.61	0.87	0.70
R7-A1	0-15	7.2	6.8	0.22	23.0	1.30	0.07	23.75	0.2	---	100	0.60	8.25	4.79	0.33	15:1	27.60	1.22	2.40
R7-B21r	15-27.5	7.1	5.8	0.12	8.3	0.30	0.07	9.03	0.07	---	97	0.20	2.11	1.22	0.08	15:1	8.98	1.19	1.26
R7-C1ox	27.5-55.5	7.5	4.1	0.19	10.1	0.36	0.15	9.03	0.02	---	100	0.20	0.97	0.56	0.05	11:1	3.27	1.70	1.40
R7-C2mox	55.5-104	8.5	0.2	0.15	37.0	0.53	0.13	3.33	21.9	---	100	0.26	0.17	0.10	0.01	10:1	2.61	0.75	0.62
R7-Cnm	104+	8.4	0.4	0.12	38.0	0.53	0.10	2.95	21.2	---	100	0.30	0.11	0.06	0.01	6:1	1.14	0.72	0.54
R8-A11	0-7.5	7.6	4.2	0.58	35.0	1.1	0.23	18.29	5.4	12.3	100	1.75	7.67	4.45	0.13	34:1	44.91	1.44	1.94
R8-A12	7.5-17.5	7.9	4.1	0.18	32.0	0.63	0.10	11.92	2.4	3.1	100	0.93	3.70	2.15	0.06	36:1	23.52	1.90	1.40
R8-B21r	17.5-35.5	8.3	1.9	0.18	34.0	0.63	0.10	7.41	11.0	23.0	100	0.58	2.02	1.17	0.08	15:1	19.11	0.79	1.05
R8-C1ox	35.5-50.5	8.5	2.2	0.12	34.0	0.36	0.09	4.94	17.9	47.8	100	0.30	1.29	0.75	0.05	15:1	14.37	1.60	0.85
R8-C2ox	50.5-96	8.5	0.3	0.09	35.0	0.30	0.10	4.51	18.6	47.8	100	0.63	1.23	0.71	0.05	14:1	3.76	1.17	0.77
R8-Cn(1)	178.5	8.7	0.2	0.09	34.0	0.43	0.15	2.61	16.8	41.8	100	0.54	tr	...	0.01	...	2.78	1.14	0.46
R8-Cn(2)	239	8.7	0.4	0.16	34.0	0.69	0.19	2.09	17.7	40.2	100	0.45	0.11	0.06	0.01	6:1	1.14	0.77	0.40

R10-A11	0-7.5	7.3	3.92	0.18	31.5	0.84	0.31	18.41	1.06	2.7	100	0.66	7.67	4.45	0.24	19:1	---	1.25	1.99
R10-A12	7.5-15	7.6	3.32	0.12	15.4	0.28	0.20	10.46	0.12	0.6	100	0.51	1.94	1.13	0.06	19:1	---	2.13	1.28
R10-B2t	15-40.5	7.9	1.81	0.19	44.2	1.0	0.22	13.58	9.19	21.8	100	0.48	0.86	0.50	0.04	13:1	---	1.78	1.17
R10-Cox	40.5-114	8.3	tr	0.11	41.6	0.71	0.25	5.73	16.5	40.3	100	0.61	0.03	0.02	0.01	2:1	---	0.98	0.54
R10-Cn	114+	8.4	tr	0.11	41.6	0.84	0.22	2.52	16.8	43.2	100	0.60	0.05	0.03	0.01	3:1	---	0.83	0.48
WD2-A1	0-20	7.8	8.8	0.11	19.6	0.53	0.09	11.26	9.3	---	100	0.31	3.76	2.18	0.14	16:1	4.41	0.54	1.15
WD2-B1r	20-27.5	7.6	8.7	0.02	4.3	0.20	0.04	3.42	0.1	---	100	0.26	0.97	0.56	0.03	19:1	7.51	0.53	0.58
WD2-C1ox	27.5-68	7.2	0.9	0.02	2.1	0.10	0.04	1.90	0.1	---	100	0.23	0.23	0.13	0.01	13:1	3.76	0.46	0.34
WD2-C2ox	68-80.5	7.6	1.9	0.11	8.3	0.25	0.09	7.03	0.2	---	100	0.31	0.51	0.30	0.02	15:1	8.00	1.58	1.01
WD2-C3ox	80.5-106	8.3	0.5	0.12	40.0	0.59	0.10	1.32	16.4	---	100	0.46	0.63	0.37	0.03	12:1	3.10	1.12	1.05
WD2-Cn	106+	8.7	0.4	0.07	37.0	0.53	0.04	2.09	21.7	---	100	0.30	0.23	0.13	0.01	13:1	3.10	0.58	0.62

a ...no detection. ---not analyzed. Soil pits (e.g. L1, R2) can be located on Figs. 3, 4, 5 and 6.

This dehydrochlorination reaction may also produce 2,2-di-chloroethylene (DDE). Laboratory dehydrochlorination rates for the p,p' isomer have been determined by Metcalf (1955) who showed that the rate of hydrolysis increased sevenfold from -7° to 3°C. Fleck and Haller (1946) showed that de-hydrochlorination proceeds more rapidly in the presence of catalysts such as Fe, Al, and Cr salts, and at normal temper-atures iron salts cause the reaction to occur at a faster rate. Technical DDT decomposes at 38°C (100°F), a process which is accelerated with maximum surface exposure (e.g. field conditions where vegetation is largely absent) and ultraviolet irradiation between 2200–2400 Å (Fleck, 1949). This reaction produces noninsecticidal compounds.

Under anaerobic conditions, soil microorganisms con-vert DDT to DDD (1,1-dichloro-2,2-bis p-chlorophenylethane) (Kaufman, 1966). The data in Table 2.6 suggest a slight in-crease of DDD and DDE from the degradation of DDT in the soil. The low concentrations at depth in most profiles result from the low solubility of DDT. The presence of DDT in the sub-surface horizons of site R6 is seen as a result of ground-water fluctuation and/or leaching from the surface into the Cm horizon where higher clay content and lower permeability combine to retain pesticides.

Dieldrin, which is present in trace amounts, results from the oxidation of aldrin according to the following equation.

$$\text{(3)}$$

Aldrin   Dieldrin

Aldrin was not detected in the natural forest soils, while dieldrin is present in trace amounts at sites R8 and R10.

Atrazine (2-chloro-4-ethylamino-6-isopropylamino-s-triazine) is present only at site WD2. Atrazine has a solubility of 70 ppm at 27° which increases to 320 ppm at $85^{o}C$ (Freed, 1966), a value much higher than DDT (1 ppb) which is hydrophobic (Weber and Weed, 1974). Talbert and Fletchall (1965) have studied the adsorption of atrazine by various exchangers under conditions of different pH. Kaolinite will not adsorb atrazine, while illite adsorbs only small quantities as it lacks the required electropositive charges necessary for attraction to the negatively charged clay surfaces. Even though atrazine was applied as a herbicide to crops in nearby fields, its low adsorption led to rapid removal from soil profiles (Table 2.6).

Conclusions

Soils in woodlots do not appear to have been affected by prehistoric or historic man to any great degree (see Chapter 5). Selective cutting may have led to thinning of forest stands and concomitant reduction in leaf-fall, organic matter, and humus. Many hardwoods in these forest stands have high diameter-breast-height ratios which indicate that the trees began growing prior to the arrival of settlers. The first settlers into the field area arrived in 1810 from Pennsylvania (see Chapter 5 for a discussion of European settlement history).

In retrospect, site L1 was probably a poor choice for a type section. Not only is it badly disturbed by housing construction, but vegetation is second growth in places, and an A/C profile is unlike that described at other sites in eastern Toronto, where the Leaside Till and soil are well-exposed. A better type section could be defined at sites R7 or R8 in the Little Rouge Creek Basin.

The post-Leaside soil under forest cover consists of an O/A/B/Cox/Cn horizon sequence with well-developed horizon contacts, a high loess component in surface horizons, and a well-developed textural and color B horizon. Effects of leaching through the solum are apparent, especially where clay and small amounts of pesticides are deposited at depth. Clay mineralogy in the natural soils indicates a weathering sequence where mixed-layer illite-montmorillonite decreases from the parent material upward into the profile giving rise

Table 2.6. Pesticide concentration for the horizons in Table 2.1.

Sample[a]	Depth (cm)	<2mm fractions (ppm)					
		p,p' DDT	o,p' DDT	DDE	DDD	Dieldrin	Atrazine
Site Horizon							
R2-A11	0-18	.013	.001	.013	.002	...	...
R2-B2t	18-46	...	...	...	...	...	...
R2-Cox	46-89	...	...	...	...	...	...
R2-Cn	89+	...	...	...	...	...	...
R6-A1	0-18	...	...	...	...	...	...
R6-A2	18-30.5	...	...	...	...	...	...
R6-B2t	30.5-68.5	.002	...	...	...	...	...
R6-Cmox	68.5-106.5	.004	tr	.002	.001	...	...
R6-Cn(1)	127	...	...	.003	tr	...	...
R6-Cn(2)	178.5	...	...	...	...	...	...
R7-A1	0-15	.016	.001	.007	.002	...	...
R7-B2ir	15-27.5	...	...	...	...	...	...
R7-C1ox	27.5-55.5	...	...	...	...	...	...
R7-C2mox	55.5-104	...	...	...	...	...	...
R7-Cnm	104+	...	...	...	...	...	...
R8-A11	0-7.5	.020	.001	.009	.003	tr	—
R8-A12	7.5-17.5	.003	tr	.004	.002	tr	—
R8-B2ir	17.5-35.5	tr	...	.002	tr	...	—
R8-C1ox	35.5-50.5	.001	...	.003	.001	tr	—
R8-C2ox	50.5-96	.001	...	.002	.001	...	—
R8-Cn(1)	178.5	tr	...	tr	tr	tr	—
R8-Cn(2)	239	tr	...	tr	tr	tr	—

62

R10-A11	0-7.5	.054	.003	.025	.005	tr	—
R10-A12	7.5-15	.005	tr	.005	.001	:	—
R10-B2t	15-40.5	.002	tr	.003	.001	tr	—
R10-Cox	40.5-114	.001	:	.002	tr	:	—
R10-Cn	114+	tr	:	.002	tr	:	—
WD2-A1	0-20	.012	tr	.008	.002	:	0.005
WD2-Bir	20-27.5	:	:	:	:	:	:
WD2-C1ox	27.5-68	:	:	:	:	:	:
WD2-C2ox	68-80.5	:	:	:	:	:	:
WD2-C3ox	80.5-106	:	:	:	:	:	:
WD2-Cn	106+	:	:	:	:	:	:

[a] ...no detection; — not analyzed. Soil pits (e.g. R2, R8) can be located on Figs. 4, 5 and 6.

63

to chlorite, halloysite, kaolinite, and illite. Pesticides
are present in small quantities in most soil profiles as a
result of degradation of DDT to DDD and DDE, oxidation of
aldrin to dieldrin, and low adsorption rates of atrazine.
However, the data indicate that pesticides applied to plowed
fields may also affect nearby forest areas.

CHAPTER 3

SOIL SYSTEMS IN CLEARED AREAS

The extent to which clearing processes have disturbed natural soils, found in association with a deciduous forest cover, is examined on the basis of soil profiles described in cleared areas.

Soil Morphology

Soils were studied in the Little Rouge and West Duffin Creek basins (Figs. 3.1, 3.2, 3.3, and 3.4), and representative profile samples were collected for laboratory study (Table 3.1). These soils are well-developed and display O/A/B/Cox/Cn horizon sequences. Excepting the O horizons, which are somewhat thinner when compared with forest soils, profiles R1 (Fig. 3.5) and WD1 (Fig. 3.6) are quite similar to profiles found in association with forest cover (Table 2.1). A horizon complexes range from 15 to 20 cm depth, B horizons vary from 18 to 35 cm thickness, and C horizons from 55 to 90 cm. Total depths of the profiles range from 98 to 153 cm. In both cases the B horizons are textural, and exhibit some evidence of clay movement (e.g. clay skins on peds). Surface soil colors are black (10YR 2/1), and merge downward with grayish-yellow brown (10YR 4/2, 4/3, 5/3) and dull yellowish-brown (10YR 4/3) material in the A horizons. Site WD1 (Fig. 3.6) has an A2 horizon with a somewhat lighter hue.

Textures in the profiles vary from loam and pebbly loam in the A horizons, pebbly clay loam, pebbly sandy loam, and loam in the B horizons, to pebbly loam in the C horizons. Structure in the A horizons ranges from granular and crumb to massive; B horizons are blocky, and C horizons blocky to massive. Moist consistence ranges from friable and firm in the A horizons, to firm in most B horizons, and to friable in the C horizons. Unconfined shear-strengths give average values (n=20) of 1.0 kg/cm^2 in A horizons, B horizons average (n=30) 1.8 kg/cm^2, and C horizons (n=40) yield values of 4.0 kg/cm^2.

The soil morphology of the profiles in cleared areas is comparable to soils forming under forest cover. Root systems generally penetrate to the base of the B horizons. B horizons are mottled with iron oxides as attested to by the range in color. Horizon boundaries are generally sharp, at

Figure 3.1. Site R1 in the Little Rouge Creek Drainage
Basin. The stream has cut through 15 m
of Leaside Till. The surface soil is an
Alfisol (high base status). For location
see Fig. 1.6.

least in the solum, and some horizons tend to exhibit un-
dulations which may result from leaching, and/or differential
freeze-thaw processes.

Particle Size

        Coarse grade-sizes (64-2 mm) are dominated by large to
medium pebbles (Table 3.2). Bulk weight-percentages show
that sand, silt, and clay dominate over coarse materials
amounting to ~90 percent of the total sample. Insofar as the
<2 mm fractions are concerned, sand and silt dominate over
clay; silt increases in the surface horizons, and clay increases in the B horizons. Analysis of grade-sizes (Table
3.3) shows that sand increases with depth in the profiles,
and dominates in the medium to very fine grade-sizes. Silt

Figure 3.2. Three typical vegetation-soil associations
in juxtaposition; site R1 (cleared area,
center), site R2 (plowed field, right),
and site R3 (forest, left). For location
see Fig. 1.6.

is dominated by the coarse and medium grade-sizes, and clay
is dominated by the fine grade-size. The granulometric compositions of horizons in each profile are given in Figs. 3.7
and 3.8. The curves indicate a close correlation between
sites of the sand-silt-clay ratios, and an overall close
correspondence to profiles forming under forest cover. A-
nomalies in the particle size are explained by variations in
the original parent material and/or eolian deposition. Relative weathering, calculated by comparing the soil horizon
curves with those for the parent material (Cn), indicate that
site WD1 shows lower overall reduction in size than site R1.

The distributions of silt and clay with depth in each
profile are given in Fig. 3.9. The higher content of silt
in the A horizons suggests eolian deposition. These distributions correlate closely with those for soils forming under

Figure 3.3. Site WD1 in the West Duffin Creek Drainage
Basin. Fifteen m of Leaside Till overlie
20 m of sand and clay of the Thorncliffe
Formation. For location see Fig. 1.8.

forest cover (Figs. 2.15 and 2.16). The particle-size classification for samples in different horizons is given in Fig.
3.10 which shows the tendency for finer size to dominate in
the B horizons.

Clay Mineralogy

        The mineralogy of the <2μ grade-size is given in Table
3.4. The data indicate that illite is the most abundant clay
mineral within the 2:1 clay-mineral suite, while kaolinite is
slightly more prevalent than halloysite in the 1:1 clay-
mineral suite. The weathering sequence suggests that halloysite and chlorite form only in the solum, while illite is
limited to the C horizon complex. Mixed-layer illite-montmorillonite is present in trace amounts through each profile
which is quite different from profiles under forest cover.

Figure 3.4. Cleared field near site WD1. The soil is untilled, but hay crop is removed every year. For location see Fig. 1.8.

69

Table 3.1. Relict soil profiles[ab] from cleared areas.

Profile: R1
Age: post-Leaside
Location: Stream cut, Little Rouge Creek.
Elevation: 183 m.
Vegetation: Grasses.
Parent Material: Till, predominantly of dolomite, limestone, shale, granitic and gneissic materials.

Soil Horizon	Depth (cm)	Description
01	0 - 2.0	Black (10YR 2/1).
A11	0 - 7.5	Grayish-yellow brown (10YR 4/2m, 10YR 4/2d) loam; granular structure; friable moist consistence; sticky and plastic; numerous medium and small roots; frequent worms and wormholes.
A12	7.5 - 15.0	Dull yellowish-brown (10YR 4/3, 10YR 4/3d) loam; massive structure; firm moist consistence; sticky and plastic: numerous medium and fine roots.
B2t	15.0 - 43.0	Dark brown (10YR 3/4m), and dull yellow-orange (10YR 6/ 3d) pebbly clay loam; block structure; firm moist consistence; sticky and plastic; numerous fine and medium roots.
B3	43.0 - 61.0	Mottled brown (10YR 4/4m) to dull yellow-orange (10YR 7/3m, 10YR 6/3d) pebbly sandy loam; blocky structure; firm moist consistence; sticky and plastic; few roots.
C1ox	61 - 117	Dull yellow-orange (10YR 7/2m, 10YR 7/3d) pebbly loam; blocky structure; firm moist consistence; sticky and plastic.
C2ox	117 - 152.5	Dull yellowish-brown (10YR 5/4m) to dull yellow-orange (10YR 7/2d) pebbly loam; massive structure; firm moist consistence; sticky and plastic.
Cn	152.5+	Yellowish-brown (2.5Y 5/3m) to light yellow (2.5Y 7/3d) pebbly loam; massive structure; firm moist consistence; sticky and slightly plastic.

Profile: WD1
Age: post-Leaside
Location: Stream cut, West Duffin Creek, Clarkes Hollow.
Elevation: 168 m.
Vegetation: Red cedar, hemlock.
Parent Material: Till and loess, predominantly of dolomite, limestone, shale and granitic materials.

Soil Horizon	Depth (cm)	Description
01	0 - 3.5	Black (10YR 2/1).
A11	0 - 7.5	Grayish-yellow brown (10YR 5/2m) and dull yellowish-brown (10YR 4/3d) loam; crumb structure; friable moist consistence; sticky and plastic; numerous fine and medium (>5mm) roots; few worms.
A12	7.5 - 15	Grayish-yellow brown (10YR 4/2m) and dull yellowish-brown (10YR 5/3d) loam; massive structure; friable moist consistence; sticky and plastic; numerous fine and medium root systems.
A2	15 - 20	Dull yellowish-brown (10YR 5/3m) and dull yellow-orange (10YR 6/4d) pebbly loam; massive structure; friable moist consistence; slightly sticky and plastic; numerous fine and medium root systems.
IIB2t	20 - 30	Mottled brown (10YR 4/4m) and dull yellowish-brown (10YR 5/4m, 10YR 5/4d) loam; blocky structure; sticky and plastic; fewer fine and plentiful medium roots.
IIB3	30 - 37.5	Mottled brown (10YR 4/4m) and dull yellow-orange (10YR 6/4m, 10YR 6/3d) loam; blocky structure; friable moist consistence; sticky and plastic.

Horizon	Depth (cm)	Description
IIC1ox	37.5 - 73	Dull yellow-orange (10YR 6/3m, 10YR 7/2d) pebbly loam; blocky structure; friable moist consistence; sticky and slightly plastic.
IIC2ox	73 - 98	Dull yellowish-brown (10YR 5/3m) and dull yellow-orange (10YR 7/3d) pebbly loam; massive structure; friable moist consistence; sticky and plastic.
IICn	98+	Olive brown (2.5Y 4/3m) and grayish-yellow (2.5Y 7/2d) pebbly loam; massive structure; friable moist consistence; sticky and plastic.

aTerms and horizon nomenclature employed are in standard use with the U.S.D.A. (1951, 1960). Soil colors are given as moist (m) and dry (d).

bSoil pit locations (e.g. R1, WD1) can be located in Figs. 4 and 6.

71

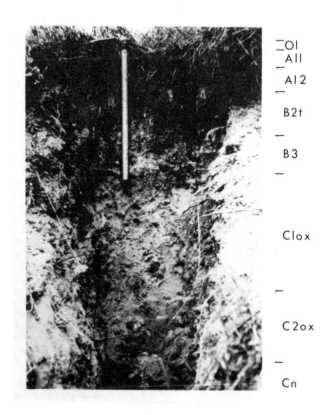

Ol
All
Al2
B2t

B3

Clox

C2ox

Cn

Figure 3.5. Soil profile R1, Little Rouge Creek
Drainage Basin. The soil is an Alfisol
(high base status). For location see
Fig. 1.6. The mattock is 68 cm.

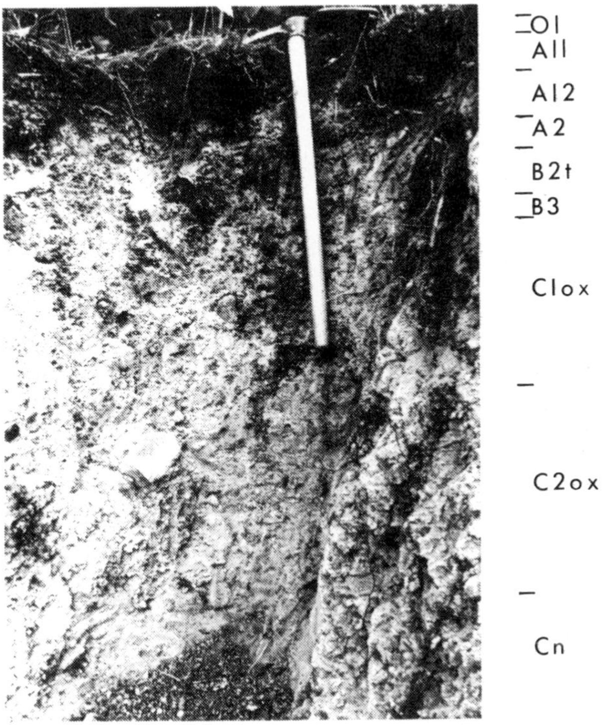
O1
A11
A12
A2
B2t
B3
C1ox
C2ox
Cn

Figure 3.6. Soil profile WD1, West Duffin Creek Drainage Basin. The soil is a Spodosol with well-developed albic and argillic horizons. For location see Fig. 1.8. The mattock is 68 cm.

Table 3.2. Particle-size distribution[a] for material >2mm in Table 3.1. The data are given in weight-percentage of dry mineral matter and bulk weight-percentage of sand, silt and clay (<2mm).

Sample[b]	Depth (cm)	Pebble Very Large 64-32 mm ($-6/-5\mu$)	Pebble Large 32-16 mm ($-5/-4\mu$)	Pebble Medium 16-8 mm ($-4/-3\mu$)	Pebble Small 8-4 mm ($-3/-2\mu$)	Granule 4-2 mm ($-2/-1\mu$)	Total Sample Pebble %	Total Sample Granule %	Total Sample Sand-Silt-Clay %	<2mm Fractions Sand %	<2mm Fractions Silt %	<2mm Fractions Clay %
Site Horizon												
R1-A11	0-7.5	...	...	...	0.1	0.1	0.1	0.1	99.8	42.8	38.6	18.6
R1-A12	7.5-15	...	...	0.2	0.7	0.7	0.9	0.7	98.4	42.9	38.1	19.0
R1-B2t	15-43	...	2.6	3.2	3.4	2.8	9.2	2.8	88.1	40.0	30.2	29.8
R1-B3	43-61	10.9	6.5	5.6	3.7	2.8	26.7	2.8	70.5	52.4	32.4	15.2
R1-C1ox	61-117	...	3.6	4.5	3.2	2.9	11.4	2.9	85.7	48.8	39.8	11.4
R1-C2ox	117-152.5	...	6.1	3.5	3.5	3.2	13.1	3.2	83.8	47.6	40.0	12.4
R1-Cn	152.5+	4.4	1.5	3.2	2.6	2.5	11.8	2.5	85.8	48.1	38.3	13.6
WD1-A11	0-7.5	...	...	0.1	0.4	0.5	0.5	0.5	99.1	41.6	41.0	17.4
WD1-A12	7.5-15	...	0.3	1.0	0.7	0.8	2.0	0.8	97.2	40.0	42.4	17.6
WD1-A2	15-20	...	0.9	1.1	1.0	1.2	3.0	1.2	95.8	41.5	40.8	17.7
WD1-B2t	20-30	...	1.5	1.0	1.1	1.3	3.6	1.3	95.1	41.4	36.7	21.9
WD1-B3	30-37.5	...	3.7	3.0	3.3	2.8	10.0	2.8	87.2	44.2	33.9	21.9
WD1-C1ox	37.5-73	...	1.4	2.9	3.0	3.2	7.3	3.2	89.5	44.0	37.1	18.9
WD1-C2ox	73-98	7.7	2.2	3.0	3.0	2.1	15.9	2.1	82.0	44.1	37.5	18.4
WD1-Cn	98+	...	0.5	2.7	2.9	3.0	6.1	3.0	90.0	44.4	36.1	19.5

[a]Coarse particle-sizes (64 mm-63μ) determined by sieving; fine particle sizes (63 - 1.95μ) determined by hydrometer; ... nil.

[b]Soil pit locations (e.g. R1, WD1) can be located on Figs. 4 and 6.

Table 3.3. Particle-size distribution[a] for material < 2mm in Table 3.1. The data are given in weight-percentage and cumulative weight-percent of dry mineral matter.

For each sample the first line gives weight-percent and the second line gives cumulative weight-percent.

Sample[b]	Depth (cm)	SAND Very Coarse 2–1 mm (−1/0φ)	SAND Coarse 1mm–500µ (0–1φ)	SAND Medium 500–250µ (1–2φ)	SAND Fine 250–125µ (2–3φ)	SAND Very Fine 125–63µ (3–4φ)	SILT Coarse 63–31.2µ (4–5φ)	SILT Medium 31.2–15.6µ (5–6φ)	SILT Fine 15.6–7.8µ (6–7φ)	SILT Very Fine 7.8–3.9µ (7–8φ)	CLAY Coarse 2.9–1.95µ (8–9φ)	CLAY Fine < 1.95µ (>9φ)
Site Horizon												
R1-A11	0–7.5	0.2	2.6	10.0	16.9	12.9	16.3	10.9	6.6	4.9	3.3	15.4
		0.2	2.8	12.9	29.8	42.8	59.1	69.9	76.5	81.4	84.7	100
R1-A12	7.5–15	.9	3.1	9.9	15.9	13.0	16.8	10.4	6.1	4.8	3.3	15.6
		.9	4.0	14.0	29.8	42.9	59.7	70.1	76.2	81.0	84.3	100
R1-B2t	15–43	1.9	3.3	9.8	14.7	10.3	12.4	7.4	5.6	4.8	3.9	25.9
		1.9	5.2	15.0	29.7	40.0	52.4	59.8	65.4	70.2	74.1	100
R1-B3	43–61	1.5	3.3	11.0	20.0	16.6	17.3	7.3	4.3	3.4	2.0	13.3
		1.5	4.8	15.8	35.8	52.4	69.7	77.1	81.4	84.8	86.7	100
R1-C1ox	61–117	1.2	3.1	10.0	18.3	16.2	20.4	10.1	5.9	3.4	2.3	9.1
		1.2	4.3	14.3	32.6	48.8	69.2	79.3	85.2	88.6	90.9	100
R1-C2ox	117–152.5	1.2	3.6	10.2	16.8	15.8	17.8	11.5	6.8	3.9	2.7	9.6
		1.2	4.8	15.0	31.8	47.6	65.4	76.8	83.7	87.6	90.3	100
R1-Cn	152.5+	1.6	3.3	9.9	17.8	15.4	18.1	9.8	6.4	3.9	2.6	11
		1.6	5.0	14.9	32.7	48.1	66.2	76.0	82.5	86.4	89.0	100
WD1-A11	0–7.5	0.7	2.4	8.1	14.9	15.5	17.4	12.0	6.9	4.7	3.3	14.1
		0.7	3.1	11.2	26.1	41.6	59.0	71.0	77.9	82.6	85.9	100
WD1-A12	7.5–15	1.5	2.9	8.2	14.7	12.8	19.1	11.2	7.1	5.0	4.2	13.5
		1.5	4.4	12.6	27.2	40.0	59.0	70.3	77.4	82.4	85.9	100
WD1-A2	15–20	1.6	3.3	8.8	14.5	13.3	17.1	11.0	7.1	5.5	4.8	12.9
		1.6	4.9	13.7	28.2	41.5	59.0	70.3	77.4	82.4	87.1	100
WD1-B2t	20–30	2.0	3.7	9.1	14.7	11.9	13.6	9.2	7.6	6.3	5.5	16.4
		2.0	5.7	14.8	29.5	41.4	55.0	64.2	71.8	78.1	83.5	100
WD1-B3	30–37.5	1.7	4.7	9.6	13.9	13.9	15.1	8.3	6.2	4.3	3.4	18.5
		1.7	6.4	16.0	29.5	43.4	59.3	67.6	73.8	78.1	81.5	100
WD1-C1ox	37.5–73	1.6	2.8	9.2	16.5	13.9	15.7	9.7	6.8	5.0	3.5	15.3
		1.6	4.4	13.6	30.1	44.0	59.7	69.3	76.2	81.1	84.7	100
WD1-C2ox	73–98	1.4	3.2	9.3	16.6	14.3	16.6	9.0	6.8	5.1	3.2	15.1
		1.4	4.7	14.0	30.1	44.1	60.7	69.7	76.5	81.6	84.8	100
WD1-Cn	98+	2.0	3.2	9.2	15.8	14.2	15.4	8.9	6.8	4.9	3.8	15.8
		2.0	5.2	14.4	30.3	44.4	59.8	68.7	75.6	80.5	84.2	100

[a] Coarse particle-sizes (2 mm–63µ) determined by sieving, fine particle-sizes (63 – 1.95µ) determined by hydrometer.

[b] Soil pits (e.g. R1, WD1) can be located on Figs. 4 and 6.

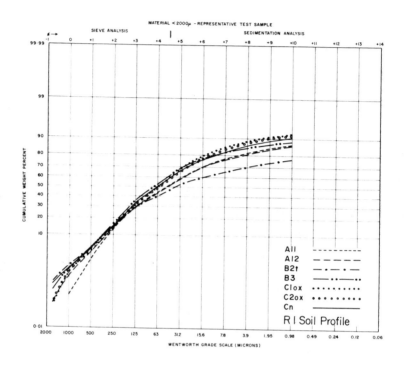

Figure 3.7.   Particle-size analysis of profile R1.

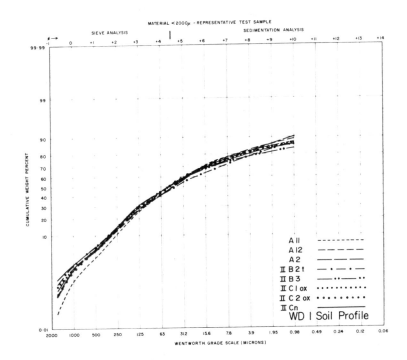

Figure 3.8. Particle-size analysis of profile WD1.

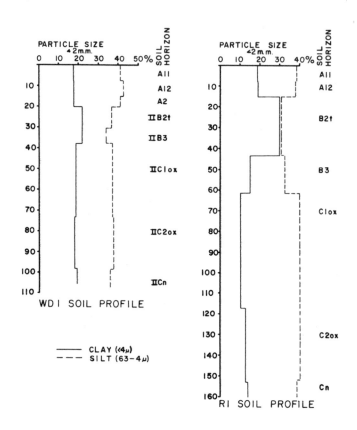

Figure 3.9. Particle-size distribution with depth for soils forming on glacial deposits in cleared areas. Soil horizon nomenclature is: B2t for textural B horizon; Cox for oxidized C horizon; and Cn for unweathered, undifferentiated and unconsolidated parent material.

78

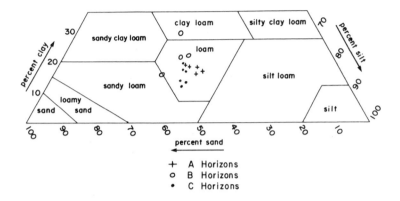

+ A Horizons
o B Horizons
• C Horizons

Figure 3.10.   Particle-size classification of soils
forming on glacial deposits. Textures
of relict soils are largely loam and
clay loam. Textural classification
follows the Soil Survey Staff (1951).

The absence of montmorillonite and the overall small quantities of 2:1 clay minerals suggests that leaching is more
efficient in removing Si^{+4} thereby reducing the Si/Al ratio.
The presence of an A2 horizon at site WD1 further substantiates the hypothesis of more powerful leaching. The relatively small percentage of kaolin minerals in the soil profiles is seen as a result of low feldspar-bearing rocks in
the parent material.

Quartz and feldspar are evenly distributed through
the profiles in an approximate ratio of 3 to 1. Calcite is
absent from profile R1, but is found in trace amount in
profile WD1.

Soil Chemistry

Soil reactions range from mildly to strongly alkaline
(Table 3.5), and the pH generally decreases upward through
the profiles. A close inverse relationship exists between
the H^+ ion (meq/100 g) and pH distributions through the

79

Table 3.4. X-ray analyses of the clay fraction (<2μ) of the horizons in
Table 3.1.

Sample[b]	Depth (cm)	Mineralogy[a]								
		Chlorite	Halloysite	Illite	Kaolinite	Montmorillonite	Mixed-Layer Illite-Montmorillonite	Feldspar	Quartz	Calcite
Site Horizon										
R1-A11	0-7.5	tr	...	tr	tr	...	tr	tr	xxx	...
R1-A12	7.5-15	tr	tr	tr	tr	...	tr	tr	xxx	...
R1-B2t	15-43	tr	tr	tr	tr	...	tr	tr	xxx	...
R1-B3	43-61	tr	tr	tr	tr	...	tr	tr	xxx	...
R1-C1ox	61-117	tr	...	tr	x	...	tr	tr	xxx	...
R1-C2ox	117-152.5	tr	...	tr	tr	...	tr	tr	xxx	...
R1-Cn	152.5+	tr	...	tr	tr	...	tr	tr	xxx	...
WD1-A11	0-7.5	tr	...	tr	tr	...	tr	tr	xxx	...
WD1-A12	7.5-15	x	...	tr	tr	...	tr	tr	xxx	...
WD1-A2	15-20	tr	tr	tr	tr	...	tr	tr	xxx	...
WD1-B2t	20-30	tr	...	tr	x	...	x	tr	xxx	...
WD1-B3	30-37.5	tr	...	tr	tr	...	tr	tr	xxx	...
WD1-C1ox	37.5-73	tr	...	tr	tr	...	tr	tr	xxx	...
WD1-C2ox	73-98	tr	...	tr	tr	???	tr	tr	xxx	...
WD1-Cn	98+	tr	...	tr	x	...	tr	tr	xxx	tr

[a] Mineral abundance is based on peak height: minor amount (tr); small amount (x); medium amount (xx); abundant (xxx); ... no detection.

[b] Soil pits (e.g. R1, WD1) can be located on Figs. 4 and 6.

Table 3.5. Selected chemical properties[a] of the <2 mm fractions of the horizons in Table 3.1.

Sample [b]	Depth (cm)	Exchangeable Cations (meq/100g)						CEC meq/100g	CaCO3 %	CO3 %	Base Sat. %	Salts mmhos/cm	O.M. %	O.C. %	N %	C:N	Fe2O3 %	Oven Dried Moisture %
		pH	H+	K+	Ca++	Mg++	Na+											
Site Horizon																		
R1-A11	0-7.5	7.5	3.56	0.24	27.0	0.76	0.07	16.66	0.81	3.0	100	0.95	5.9	3.42	0.25	14:1	1.62	1.58
R1-A12	7.5-15	7.8	2.96	0.11	27.0	0.46	0.07	13.18	0.98	2.8	100	0.55	3.4	1.97	0.16	12:1	1.43	1.34
R1-B2t	15-43	8.2	1.48	0.21	47.0	0.69	0.10	11.42	10.28	26.7	100	0.40	7.0	4.06	0.05	81:1	1.43	1.19
R1-B3	43-61	8.3	0.89	0.08	37.0	0.46	0.10	4.31	11.93	32.9	100	0.36	0.69	0.40	0.03	13:1	0.92	0.64
R1-C1ox	61-117	8.6	0.30	0.05	40.0	0.53	0.09	2.01	17.07	41.6	100	0.23	0.16	0.09	0.01	9:1	0.56	0.36
R1-C2ox	117-152.5	8.6	...	0.05	40.0	0.53	0.09	2.45	16.87	42.2	100	0.34	0.21	0.12	0.01	12:1	0.69	0.36
R1-Cn	152.5+	8.5	...	0.05	40.0	0.59	0.10	4.41	18.66	42.8	100	0.30	0.05	0.03	0.01	3:1	0.68	0.36
WD1-A11	0-7.5	7.7	2.37	0.22	29.0	0.63	0.10	11.27	1.15	3.0	100	0.68	3.5	2.03	0.16	13:1	1.52	1.24
WD1-A12	7.5-15	7.9	2.57	0.12	23.0	0.46	0.10	10.89	0.73	2.1	100	0.50	2.2	1.28	0.11	12:1	1.62	1.19
WD1-A2	15-20	7.6	2.47	0.09	17.5	0.30	0.09	53.75	0.57	1.3	33.5	0.39	1.7	0.99	0.08	12:1	1.81	1.15
WD1-B2t	20-30	7.9	2.96	0.22	29.0	0.46	0.13	14.50	0.60	1.6	100	0.37	0.96	0.56	0.05	11:1	2.95	1.73
WD1-B3	30-37.5	8.2	0.69	0.12	40.0	0.53	0.10	5.85	12.77	31.4	100	0.38	0.58	0.34	0.03	11:1	1.43	0.85
WD1-C1ox	37.5-73	8.5	...	0.07	37.0	0.53	0.10	3.30	18.06	43.2	100	0.35	0.37	0.21	0.01	21:1	0.86	0.50
WD1-C2ox	73-98	8.5	...	0.07	40.0	0.59	0.47	2.84	18.46	45.0	100	0.40	...	tr	0.01	1:1	0.88	0.48
WD1-Cn	98+	8.5	...	0.09	43.0	0.69	0.13	2.92	18.36	44.4	100	0.37	0.32	0.19	0.01	19:1	0.78	0.44

a ... no detection.

b Soil pits (e.g. R1, WD1) can be located on Figs. 4 and 6.

profiles, where H^+ ions increase in the surface horizons. Overall pH in the surface horizons is slightly higher ($\sim$0.2) in cleared than in forested areas (see Table 2.5). The mobile cations Na^+ and Ca^{+2} are lower in the solum of soils in cleared areas than in soils under forest cover, a factor attributed to slightly higher leaching in cleared areas. Exchangeable cations K^+ and Mg^{+2} have similar trends in the profiles of forested and cleared areas. Total cation exchange capacity is slightly lower in the surface horizons of soils in cleared areas probably due to the lower humus content. Calcium carbonate increases downward in the profile, reflecting a higher pH and nearness to the calcite-rich parent material. Similarly, CO_3^{-2} increases with depth in the profiles.

Base saturation reflects the degree to which the adsorption complex of a soil is saturated with exchangeable basic cations. The data shown in Table 3.5 are similar to that for forest soils. The A2 horizon at site WD1 has a base saturation of 33.5 percent which further substantiates the argument for a slightly higher degree of leaching. Salts, as products of the reaction of bases with acids, are higher in the surface horizons where pH is lower. Organic matter tends to decrease with depth in profile WD1, and shows a secondary maximum in the B2t horizon of profile R1. Similar trends for organic carbon and nitrogen are also apparent; the secondary organic matter concentration at site R1 is apparent from the high C:N ratio. Free iron oxide ranges from 0.5 to 2.95 percent. Moisture retention decreases with depth in the profiles.

Pesticides

The data for the distribution of pesticides in the profiles are presented in Table 3.6. The concentrations of p,p'DDT is somewhat smaller than in forest covered profiles (Table 2.6) while o,p'DDT is similar or slightly higher in cleared fields. The lower overall concentrations of DDT in cleared fields may result from accelerated decomposition with maximum surface exposure, higher temperatures, and a higher incidence of ultraviolet radiation between 2200–2400 $\overset{\circ}{A}$. DDT further degrades into DDD and DDE (as well as non-insecticidal compounds), which is apparent in those horizons where DDD and DDE are at higher levels than DDT. Dieldrin is present in trace amounts at site R1; the presence of this compound in the Cn horizon is either a result of groundwater fluctuation or leaching in the profile. Atrazine is not

Table 3.6. Pesticide concentration for the horizons in Table 3.1.

Sample[a]	Depth (cm)	<2 mm fractions (ppm)				
		p,p' DDT	o,p'DDT	DDE	DDD	Dieldrin
Site Horizon						
R1-A11	0-7.5	.005	tr	.004	.002	tr
R1-A12	7.5-15	.002	tr	.003	.001	...
R1-B2t	15-43	...	...	tr	tr	...
R1-B3	43-61	.001	...	.002	tr	...
R1-C1ox	61-117	...	...	tr	...	...
R1-C2ox	117-152.5	tr	...	tr	...	...
R1-Cn	152.5+	tr	...	tr	tr	tr
WD1-A11	0-7.5	.003	tr	.002	.001	...
WD1-A12	7.5-15	.001	...	.002	tr	...
WD1-A2	15-20	tr	...	.001	tr	...
WD1-B2t	20-30	tr	...	.001	tr	...
WD1-B3	30-37.5	tr	...	tr	tr	...
WD1-C1ox	37.5-73	tr	...	tr	tr	...
WD1-C2ox	73-98	tr	...	.002	tr	...
WD1-Cn	98+	.001	...	.001	tr	...

a ... no detection. Soil pits (e.g. R1, WD1) can be located
on Figs. 4 and 6.

83

present in the profiles.

Conclusions

Soils in the cleared areas are similar in most details to soils in the forested areas. However, clearing of the forest cover reduces the overall organic matter input which produces minor changes in morphology, particle size, clay mineralogy, and soil chemistry. The soil morphology, although similar to profiles under forest cover, has thinner O horizons, and less organic litter. Similarly, the hue is lighter in the A horizons of soils in cleared areas, a function of lower amounts of organic matter. A horizons, equally well-developed in both areas, are thinner in cleared areas as a result of lower amounts of organic matter input.

The textural profiles have well-developed textural B horizons which indicate at least moderate leaching. The particle-size distribution for individual horizons also indicates finer texture in the B horizons. The overall reduction in 2:1 and 2:1:1 clay minerals when compared with soils under forest cover also suggests a somewhat higher leaching power in soils in cleared areas.

Soil chemistry in the soils shows slightly higher pH and lower overall organic matter. Lower concentrations of the mobile cations Na^+ and Ca^{+2} in surface horizons indicate that leaching into the subsurface is more powerful in the cleared areas as trees are not available to intercept rainfall, and fewer humus colloids are available to retain soil moisture (e.g. lower percent oven-dried moisture, Table 3.5).

Lower overall concentrations of pesticides in soils in cleared fields suggest that pesticide degradation proceeds more quickly in open environments where ultraviolet radiation can reach the ground surface. Furthermore the overall low concentrations of pesticides indicate that DDT and other organochlorides are not long-lived in both forest and open-area environments.

CHAPTER 4

AGRICULTURAL SOILS

This chapter deals with agricultural soils that have
been tilled for more than a century. With the exception
of site R9, these soil systems have the same macroclimatic,
topographic, lithologic, and age-relationships as the soils
in cleared areas and under natural forest. Differences in
soil profile characteristics are the result of changes in
biota induced by agriculture. Pedon descriptions, particle-
size distributions, and routine analytical data are used
to analyze the effects of deep tillage on podzolic soils.

Soil Morphology

Soils affected by tillage were studied in the Rouge
River and Little Rouge Creek drainage basins and representative samples were collected for standard laboratory analysis.
Three sites are on undulating ground moraine consisting of
Leaside Till, while site R9 is on lacustrine sediments of
Iroquois age. These sites are similar in drainage and morpho-
metrical characteristics to sites described in Chapters 2
and 3 (Figs. 4.1 and 4.2). Agricultural soil horizons merge
with the soils in the ecotone zone along the forest edge
(Figs. 4.3 and 4.4) where soil morphology, particle size,
and soil chemistry relations change abruptly. Second growth
of grasses and sedges in areas formerly under tillage (Fig.
4.5) produces changes in the thickness and biochemical relationships in the A horizon complex.

Agricultural soils are well-developed with A/B/Cox/Cn
horizon sequences (Figs. 4.6, 4.7, and 4.8) as described in
Table 4.1. O horizons are not present in the soils, and A
horizons range from 19 to 31 cm in depth, B horizons from
12 to 30 cm thickness, and C horizons from 22 to 50 cm.
Total soil depth ranges from 63 to 110 cm. Horizon boundaries are sharp, and nearly parallel with the ground surface.
Colors are generally lighter than in the A horizon complex
of natural forest soils (Table 2.1), and have dark brown
(10YR 3/4), brownish-black (10YR 2/3, 2/2), and brown (10YR
4/4) hues. B horizons are brown (10YR 4/4, 7.5YR 4/3),
dull yellowish-brown (10YR 5/4), and dull yellow orange
(10YR 6/3), while C horizons are mottled dark brown (10YR
3/4), dull yellowish-brown (10YR 5/3, 5/4), dull yellow
orange (10YR 6/3, 6/4), and grayish-yellow brown (10YR 6/2).

The parent material is generally yellowish-brown (2.5Y 5/3), grayish-yellow (2.5Y 7/2), dull yellow orange (10YR 6/3), and dull yellow (2.5Y 6/4).

Textures in the A horizons are pebbly loam and loam, and they are generally finer than textures in A horizons of soils in forested areas. B horizons are clay loam, pebbly clay loam, and silty clay, while C horizons are pebbly loam, and clay. The parent material is generally pebbly loamy sand, pebbly loam, pebbly silt loam, loam and clay. Structures in the plowed surface horizons are massive (Fig. 4.8), while fallow sites (e.g., site R4, Fig. 4.9) develop greater differentiation of A horizons, and weak granular structure. B horizons have weak blocky structure, while C horizons are generally massive. Moist consistence in the A horizons is usually firm, B horizons are firm to

Figure 4.1. Undulating ground moraine consisting of
            Leaside Till, Little Rouge Creek Drainage
            Basin, site R5: corn stubble (foreground),
            grass (middleground), and corn and stand
            of mixed-hardwoods (background). For
            location see Fig. 1.6.

Figure 4.2. Ground moraine consisting of Leaside Till, incised by a small first order stream. Higher topographic positions are lighter in hue, and dryer. For location see Fig. 1.6.

Figure 4.3. Forest-edge complex of mixed-hardwoods
and tilled field at site R5. Farm
vehicles ridge and compact the soil increasing bulk density and runoff. For
location see Fig. 1.6.

Figure 4.4.   Corn stubble and forest ecotone at site R4, Little Rouge
Creek Drainage Basin. The house (center-left) is on a
10-acre site, fallow since 1967. For location see Fig. 1.6.

Figure 4.5. Fallow field (foreground), cornfield
(middleground), and forest (background)
at sites R3 and R4. For location see
Fig. 1.6.

very firm, and C horizons are firm to very firm. A horizons
are sticky and plastic, and generally lack appreciable root
systems. B horizons range from very sticky and plastic to
sticky and plastic, while C horizons are slightly sticky
and plastic to sticky and plastic, reflecting the lower
quantity of clay. Unconfined shear-strengths average (n=40)
3.45 kg/cm^2 in the A horizons, 3.25 kg/cm^2 in the B horizons (n=40), and +4.5 kg/cm^2 (n=80) in the C horizons.
Changes in physical properties as a result of plowing in
sandy loam soils are similar to results obtained by Bouma
(1969), Kondrat'yev and Gritsenko (1971) and Low (1973).

Ap

B2ir

Clox

C2ox

Cn

Figure 4.6. Soil profile in a plowed field (site R5).
Root systems penetrate to the base of the
Ap (dark surface horizon), and corn
stubble is found throughout the surface
horizon. For location see Fig. 1.6. The
mattock is 68 cm.

Ap

B2ir

Cox

Cn

Figure 4.7.   Soil profile in a plowed field (site R3).
The soil has a typical Ap surface hori-
zon, and a sharp boundary along the B
horizon contact.   For location see Fig.
1.6.   The mattock is 68 cm.

Ap

B2ir

Figure 4.8. Ap horizon of profile R3. The massive
structure and low pore space are characteristic of plowed horizons. For
location see Fig. 1.6. The knife is
24 cm.

Earthworms

Earthworms are not as prevalent in surface horizons
as they are in natural soils under forest cover. The
earthworm count in forest soils reaches $50-100/m^2$, which is
similar to data reported by Russell (1955), Gilyarvo (1942),
and Low (1972). Fecal pellets are commonly between 10-90
tons/ha. The importance of earthworms along with humus
and basic constituents in creating a mechanically stable
structure is well documented (Levin, 1969).

Table 4.1. Agriculturally modified soil profiles.[a,b]

Profile: R3
Age: post-Leaside
Location: 75 m west of site R2.
Elevation: 185 m.
Vegetation: Corn.
Parent Material: Till, predominantly of limestone, dolomite, shale, granitic and gneissic materials.

Soil Horizon	Depth (cm)	Description
Ap	0 – 28	Brownish-black (10YR 2/3m) to dull yellow-orange (10YR 6/3d) loam; massive structure; firm moist consistence; sticky and plastic; horizon boundary abrupt and undulatory; numerous corn stalks; few roots.
B2ir	28 – 40.5	Brown (10YR 4/4m), dull yellowish-brown (10YR 4/3d) clay loam; weak blocky structure; very firm moist consistence; very sticky and very plastic.
Cox	40.5 – 63.5	Dull yellow orange (10YR 6/4m, 10YR 7/3d) loam; massive structure; firm moist consistence; sticky and plastic.
Cn	63.5+	Dull yellow orange (10YR 7/3m, 10YR 7/2d) pebbly silt loam; massive structure; firm moist consistence; slightly sticky and plastic.

Profile: R4
Age: post-Leaside
Location: 50 m west of site R3.
Elevation: 185 m.
Vegetation: Grasses.
Parent Material: Till and loess, predominantly of dolomite, limestone, shale, granitic and gneissic materials.

Soil Horizon	Depth (cm)	Description
A11	0 – 11.5	Brownish-black (10YR 3/2m) to dull yellowish-brown (10YR 5/3d) pebbly loam, weak granular structure; firm moist consistence; sticky and plastic; few small roots (<2mm); few worms.
A12	11.5 – 19	Dark brown (10YR 3/4m) to dull yellowish-brown (10YR 5/3d) loam; weak granular structure; firm moist consistence; sticky and plastic; few small root systems; few worms.
B2t	19 – 45.5	Brown (10YR 4/4m) to dull yellowish-brown (10YR 5/4d) clay loam; weak blocky structure; firm moist consistence; sticky and plastic.
C1ox	45.5 – 57	Dull yellow orange (10YR 6/3m, 10YR 6/3d) loam; very weak blocky structure; firm moist consistence; sticky and plastic.
C2ox	57 – 67	Dull yellowish-brown (10YR 5/3m) to dull yellow orange (10YR 7/3d) loam; weak blocky structure; firm moist consistence; sticky and plastic.
Cn(1)	67+	Dull yellow (2.5Y 6/4m, 2.5Y 6/3d) and light gray (2.5Y 8/2d) pebbly loamy sand; massive structure; slightly sticky and plastic. Sample collected at 70 cm depth.
Cn(2)		Yellowish-brown (2.5Y 5/4m) and light yellow (2.5Y 7/3d) pebbly loam; massive structure; slightly sticky and plastic. Sample collected at 85 cm depth.

Profile: R5

Age: post-Leaside

Location: 300 m north of Steeles Avenue, 200 m west of Petticoat Creek.

Elevation: 187 m.

Vegetation: Corn.

Parent Material: Till, predominantly of limestone, dolomite, shale, and gneissic materials.

Soil Horizon	Depth (cm)	Description
Ap	0 - 30.5	Dark brown (10YR 3/4m), dull yellowish-brown (10YR 5/3d) pebbly loam, weak granular structure; firm moist consistence; sticky and plastic; few small fibrous roots and corn stalks.
B21ir	30.5 - 58.5	Mottled brown (10YR 4/4m) dull yellow orange (10YR 6/4d) pebbly clay loam; weak blocky structure; very firm moist consistence; very sticky and plastic; small roots penetrate to base of the horizon.
C1ox	58.5 - 84	Mottled dark brown (10YR 3/4m), dull yellow orange (10YR 6/4m) and dull yellowish-brown (10YR 5/4d) loam; massive structure; very firm moist consistence; very sticky and plastic.
C2ox	84 - 109.5	Mottled dull yellowish-brown (10YR 5/4m), dull yellow orange (10YR 6/3d) pebbly loam; massive structure; firm to very firm moist consistence; very sticky and plastic.
Cn(1)	109.5+	Yellowish-brown (2.5Y 5/3m) and grayish-yellow (2.5Y 7/2d) loam; massive structure; firm to very firm moist consistence; very sticky and plastic. Sample collected at 122 cm.
Cn(2)		Yellowish-brown (2.5Y 5/3m) and grayish-yellow (2.5Y 7/2d) loam; massive structure; firm to very firm moist consistence; very sticky and plastic. Sample collected at 183 cm.

Profile: R9

Age: post-Leaside

Location: 20 m north of Plug Hat Road; 400 m east of the Rouge River.

Elevation: 153 m.

Vegetation: Cornfield.

Parent Material: Lacustrine clay and loess, predominantly of dolomite and shale materials.

Soil Horizon	Depth (cm)	Description
Ap	0 - 23	Brownish-black (10YR 2/2m) and grayish yellow brown (10YR 5/2d) loam; massive structure; friable moist consistence; sticky and plastic; few small and medium roots.
B21ir	23 - 53.5	Brown (7.5YR 4/3m) and dull yellow orange (10YR 6/3d) silty clay; weak blocky structure; firm moist consistence; sticky and plastic; clay films common on peds; few small roots.
IICox	53.5 - 79	Grayish-yellow brown (10YR 6/2m) and dull yellow orange (10YR 7/2d) clay; massive to weak blocky structure; firm to very firm moist consistence; very sticky and plastic; few small roots.
IICn	79+	Dull yellow orange (10YR 6/3m) and grayish-yellow (2.5Y 7/2d) clay; massive structure; very firm moist consistence; very sticky and plastic.

[a] Terms and horizon nomenclature employed are in standard use with the U.S.D.A. (1951, 1960). Soil colors are given as moist (m) and dry (d).

[b] Soil pit locations (e.g. R3, R9) can be located on Figs. 4 and 5.

All

Al2

B2t

Clox

C2ox

Figure 4.9.   A horizon complex in a fallow field
(profile R4).   Clay skins are present
in the B horizon.   For location see
Fig. 1.6.   The knife is 24 cm.

Particle Size

Coarse grade-size distributions are dominated by
medium to small pebbles (Table 4.2).   The >2 mm fractions
amount to 15 percent or less of the bulk weight-percentages.
Pebbles and granules increase with depth in the soil profiles, ranging from 1 to ~ 15 percent.   The less-than-2 mm
fractions of sand, silt and clay range from 85 percent to
nearly 100 percent.   Sand and silt dominate in the <2 mm

Table 4.2. Particle-size distribution[a] for material >2mm in Table 4.1. The data are given in weight-percentage of dry mineral matter and bulk weight-percentage of sand, silt and clay (<2mm).

Sample[b]	Depth (cm)	Pebble Very Large 64-32 mm (-6/-5μ)	Pebble Large 32-16 mm (-5/-4μ)	Pebble Medium 16-8 mm (-4/-3μ)	Pebble Small 8-4 mm (-3/-2μ)	Granule 4-2 mm (-2/-1μ)	Pebble %	Granule %	Total Sample Sand-Silt-Clay %	<2mm Fractions Sand %	<2mm Fractions Silt %	<2mm Fractions Clay %
Site Horizon												
R3-Ap	0-28	...	1.8	0.1	0.7	1.0	2.6	1.0	96.3	36.5	37.5	26.0
R3-B2ir	28-40.5	...	1.0	1.4	1.1	0.9	3.5	0.9	95.6	39.6	33.4	27.0
R3-Cox	40.5-63.5	...	0.6	1.4	2.3	2.5	4.3	2.5	93.2	51.1	39.4	9.5
R3-Cn	63.5+	...	4.0	3.6	2.4	2.1	10.0	2.1	87.9	42.0	52.0	6.0
R4-All	0-11.5	...	0.5	0.1	0.5	0.9	1.1	0.9	98.0	36.1	39.9	24.0
R4-Al2	11.5-19	...	...	0.3	0.6	0.9	0.9	0.9	98.2	35.8	41.2	23.0
R4-B2t	19-45.5	...	...	0.3	0.4	0.7	0.7	0.7	98.6	36.4	34.6	29.0
R4-Clox	45.5-57	...	2.5	3.5	2.7	2.1	8.7	2.1	89.2	44.9	41.6	13.5
R4-C2ox	57-67	2.5	0.4	2.8	3.0	2.1	8.7	2.1	89.2	51.8	36.2	12.0
R4-Cn(1)	70	...	1.1	0.8	0.9	2.7	2.8	2.7	94.5	86.4	10.6	3.0
R4-Cn(2)	85	...	6.5	3.3	3.0	2.6	12.8	2.6	84.6	43.6	37.4	19.0
R5-Ap	0-30.5	...	1.0	1.9	1.8	1.1	4.7	1.1	94.2	40.4	36.6	23.0
R5-B2ir	30.5-58.5	...	1.2	1.1	1.6	1.5	3.9	1.5	94.6	41.6	31.4	27.0
R5-Clox	58.5-84	...	2.8	1.7	1.7	1.2	6.2	1.2	92.6	39.9	35.6	24.5
R5-C2ox	84-109.5	...	3.1	3.6	3.4	2.8	10.1	2.8	87.1	41.3	32.7	26.0
R5-Cn(1)	122	4.6	5.6	4.0	2.6	2.5	16.8	2.5	80.7	39.7	33.3	27.0
R5-Cn(2)	183	2.6	2.4	5.5	2.9	2.6	13.4	2.6	84.0	39.5	34.5	26.0
R9-Ap	0-23	...	...	0.2	0.5	0.4	0.7	0.4	98.9	28.4	47.1	24.5
R9-B2ir	23-53.5	...	...	...	0.2	0.4	0.2	0.4	99.4	9.1	42.9	48.0
R9-Cox	53.5-79	...	...	...	0.3	0.4	0.3	0.4	99.3	1.2	28.8	70.0
R9-Cn	79+	...	...	...	0.1	0.1	0.1	0.1	99.8	1.2	30.8	68.0

[a] Coarse particle-sizes (64 mm-63μ) determined by sieving; fine particle-sizes (63 - 1.95μ) determined by hydrometer; ... nil.

[b] Soil pit locations (e.g. R3, R4) can be located on Figs. 4 and 5.

97

Table 4.3. Particle-size distribution[a] for material <2mm in Table 4.1. The data are given in weight-percentage and cumulative weight-percent of dry mineral matter.

Sample[b] Site Horizon	Depth (cm)	Very Coarse 2-1 mm (-1/0Ø)	Coarse 1mm-500µ (0-1Ø)	Medium 500-250µ (1-2Ø)	Fine 250-125µ (2-3Ø)	Very Fine 125-63µ (3-4Ø)	Coarse 63-31.2µ (4-5Ø)	Medium 31.2-15.6µ (5-6Ø)	Fine 15.6-7.8µ (6-7Ø)	Very Fine 7.8-3.9µ (7-8Ø)	Coarse 2.9-1.95µ (8-9Ø)	Fine <1.95µ (79Ø)
		SAND					**SILT**				**CLAY**	
R3-Ap	0-28	1.56	2.90	7.76	12.60	11.64	9.54	12.5	7.0	8.5	6.0	20.0
		1.56	4.46	12.22	24.82	36.46	46.0	58.5	65.5	74.0	80.0	100
R3-B2ir	28-40.5	1.28	2.90	8.16	13.60	13.90	10.36	10.0	7.0	6.0	3.0	24.0
		1.28	3.98	12.14	25.74	39.64	50.0	60.0	67.0	73.0	76.0	100
R3-Cox	40.5-63.5	3.28	4.96	10.66	15.56	16.66	11.88	10.5	8.5	8.5	4.5	5.0
		3.28	8.24	18.90	34.46	51.12	63.0	73.5	82.0	90.5	95.0	100
R3-Cn	63.5+	4.12	4.36	6.26	8.44	18.86	23.96	14.0	9.5	4.5	1.5	4.5
		4.12	8.48	14.74	23.18	42.04	66.0	80.0	89.5	94.0	95.5	100
R4-Al1	0-11.5	1.46	2.70	7.46	12.42	12.10	10.36	15.5	8.0	6.0	7.5	16.5
		1.46	4.16	11.62	24.04	36.14	46.5	62.0	70.0	76.0	83.5	100
R4-Al2	11.5-19	1.36	2.54	7.16	12.64	12.14	10.16	16.0	10.0	5.0	3.5	19.5
		1.36	3.90	11.06	23.70	35.84	46.0	62.0	72.0	77.0	80.5	100
R4-B2t	19-45.5	.86	1.70	6.48	12.80	14.56	11.6	13.0	7.0	3.0	5.0	24.0
		.86	2.56	9.04	21.84	36.40	48.0	61.0	68.0	71.0	76.0	100
R4-Clox	45.5-57	1.74	4.28	9.02	14.94	14.90	15.12	12.0	8.5	6.0	5.3	8.2
		1.74	6.02	15.04	29.98	44.88	60.0	72.0	80.5	86.5	91.8	100
R4-C2ox	57-67	3.32	5.40	12.90	17.12	13.08	7.18	11.0	9.0	9.0	4.0	8.0
		3.32	8.72	21.62	38.74	51.82	59.0	70.0	79.0	88.0	92.0	100
R4-Cn(1)	70	3.70	13.02	30.64	25.04	14.00	5.6	3.0	1.2	0.8	0.0	3.0
		3.70	16.72	47.36	72.40	86.40	92.0	95.0	96.2	97.0	97.0	100
R4-Cn(2)	85	2.74	4.96	9.84	13.80	12.22	6.44	11.0	10.0	10.0	4.0	15.0
		2.74	7.70	17.54	31.34	43.56	50.0	61.0	71.0	81.0	85.0	100
R5-Ap	0-30.5	3.22	3.96	8.70	13.02	11.46	10.64	9.5	9.5	7.0	6.0	17.0
		3.22	7.18	15.88	28.90	40.36	51.0	60.5	70.0	77.0	83.0	100
R5-B2ir	30.5-58.5	3.28	4.26	9.04	13.22	11.80	10.40	8.0	6.5	6.5	4.0	23.0
		3.28	7.54	16.58	29.80	41.60	52.0	60.0	66.5	73.0	77.0	100
R5-Clox	58.5-84	2.52	3.70	8.70	12.96	12.00	10.12	10.5	8.5	6.5	4.0	20.5
		2.52	6.22	14.92	27.88	39.88	50.0	60.5	69.0	75.5	79.5	100

Sample	Depth											
R5-C2ox	84–109.5	2.48	4.50	9.28	13.34	11.70	10.70	9.0	6.0	7.0	7.5	18.5
		2.48	6.98	16.26	29.60	41.30	52.0	61.0	67.0	74.0	81.5	100
R5-Cn(1)	122	3.28	4.64	8.48	12.28	11.02	8.8	8.0	8.5	8.0	7.0	20.0
		3.28	7.92	16.40	28.68	39.70	48.5	56.5	65.0	73.0	80.0	100
R5-Cn(2)	183	3.80	4.76	8.84	11.78	10.36	8.46	8.0	9.0	9.0	6.0	20.0
		3.80	8.56	17.40	29.18	39.54	48.0	56.0	65.0	74.0	80.0	100.00
R9-Ap	0–23	0.94	3.12	8.84	9.30	6.22	9.58	18.0	10.0	9.5	6.5	18.0
		0.94	4.06	12.90	22.20	28.42	38.0	56.0	66.0	75.5	82.0	100
R9-B2ir	23–53.5	0.68	1.22	2.90	2.46	1.88	3.86	11.0	14.0	14.0	11.0	37.0
		0.68	1.90	4.80	7.26	9.14	13.0	24.0	38.0	52.0	63.0	100
R9-Cox	53.5–79	0.16	0.12	0.12	0.30	0.54	1.46	3.5	9.8	14.0	17.0	53.0
		0.16	0.28	0.40	0.70	1.24	2.7	6.2	16.0	30.0	47.0	100
R9-Cn	79+	0.10	0.16	0.24	0.36	0.36	0.58	1.2	7.5	21.5	19.0	49.0
		0.10	0.26	0.50	0.86	1.22	1.8	3.0	10.5	32.0	51.0	100

a Coarse particle-sizes (2 mm – 63μ) determined by sieving; fine particle-sizes (63 – 1.95μ) determined by hydrometer.

b Soil pits (e.g. R3, R4) can be located on Figs. 4 and 5.

fractions, excepting site R9 where silt and clay dominate (lacustrine sediment). Generally the solum has greater concentrations of clay when compared with the parent material. Silt is dominated by the medium and fine fractions, while sand concentrates in the medium to fine fractions. Curves showing the granulometric compositions of the horizons in each profile are shown in Figs. 4.10, 4.11, 4.12, and 4.13. The subsurface horizons correlate fairly closely with soils formed under forest cover or in cleared areas, while the A and B horizons tend to have higher percentages of clay. The tendency for rotary implements to comminute mineral material has been documented by several workers (Fiskell and Calvert, 1975; Soane and Pidgeon, 1975).

The distributions of silt and clay with depth in the profiles are shown in Fig. 4.14, indicating some clay illuviation, and a general absence of loess in the surface horizons. Profile R9 is the only soil with high silt in the surface horizons. The particle-size classification is given in Fig. 4.15.

Clay Mineralogy

The mineralogy of the $<2\mu$ grade size is given in Table 4.4. The data indicate a weathering sequence where mixed-layer illite-montmorillonite recrystallizes to form illite, montmorillonite, chlorite, kaolinite, and halloysite. Within the 2:1 clay-mineral suite, illite tends to concentrate in the lower solum and Cox horizons, while montmorillonite is present in trace amount in the surface horizon of site R4. Leaching tends to lower the Si/Al ratio making it difficult for 2:1 clay minerals to form. Insofar as the 2:1:1 clay minerals are concerned, chlorite increases with depth in the profiles, but it is not generally present in the parent material. The 1:1 clay mineral suite, consisting of kaolinite and halloysite, tends to concentrate in the surface horizons where lower pH and higher H^+ ion concentration create a moderate leaching environment.

The quartz-feldspar ratio is generally 3:1 with quartz tending to decrease with depth in the profiles. Calcite concentrates in the parent material and Cox horizons.

The data suggest a weathering sequence similar to that in soils forming under natural forest and in cleared areas. Further, the data for plowed soils indicate a higher degree of leaching and lower amounts of 2:1 clay minerals.

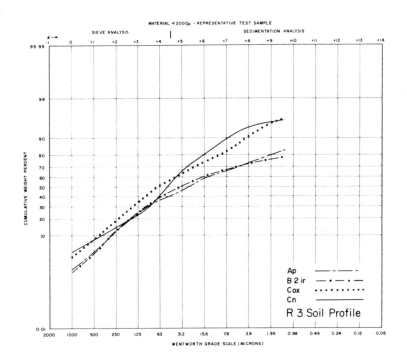

Figure 4.10. Particle-size analysis of profile R3.

101

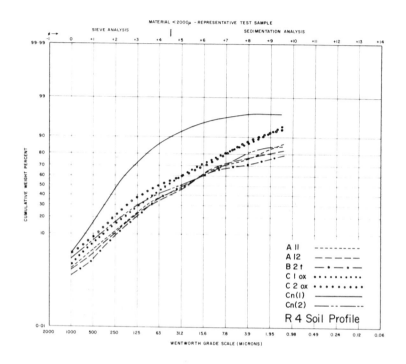

MATERIAL < 2000μ - REPRESENTATIVE TEST SAMPLE

Figure 4.11.   Particle-size analysis of profile R4.

102

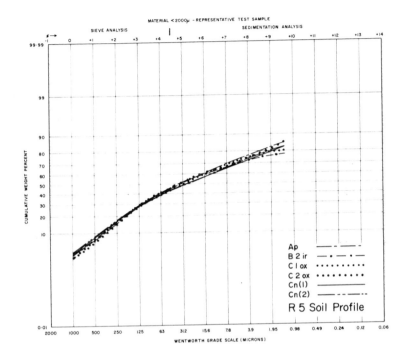

Figure 4.12. Particle-size analysis of profile R5.

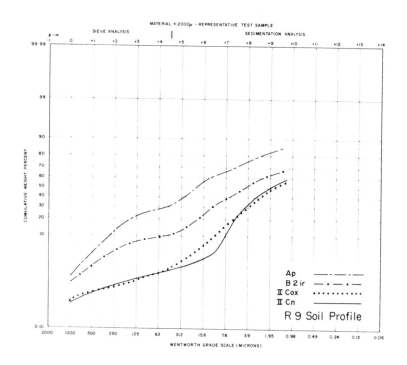

Figure 4.13.   Particle-size analysis of profile R9.

104

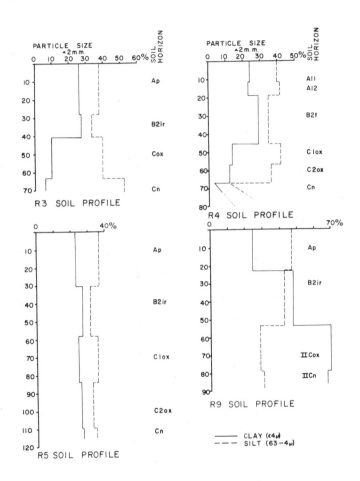

Figure 4.14.   Particle-size distribution with depth
for soils forming on Leaside Till and
lacustrine sediment of Iroquois age.
Soil nomenclature is Bir for color B
horizon; Bt for textural B horizon;
Cox for oxidized C horizon; and Cn for
unweathered, unconsolidated, and undifferentiated parent material.

105

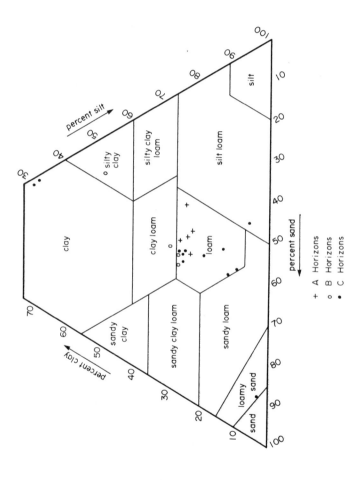

Figure 4.15. Particle-size classification of soils forming on glacial and lacustrine deposits. Textures of relict soils vary from loamy sand, loam, silt loam, to clay. The average particle size is loam. The textural classification follows the Soil Survey Staff (1951).

106

Table 4.4. X-ray analyses of the clay fraction (< 2µ) of the horizons in Table 4.1.

Sample [b]	Depth (cm)	Mineralogy [a]								
		Chlorite	Halloysite	Illite	Kaolinite	Montmorillonite	Mixed-Layer Illite-Montmorillonite	Feldspar	Quartz	Calcite
Site Horizon										
R3-Ap	0-28	tr	...	tr	tr	...	tr	tr	xxx	...
R3-B2ir	28-40.5	x	...	x	tr	...	x	tr	xx	...
R3-Cox	40.5-63.5	...	...	tr	...	...	x	tr	x	xxx
R3-Cn	63.5+	...	...	tr	...	...	xx	tr	x	xxx
R4-A11	0-11.5	x	tr	x	tr	tr	x	x	xx	...
R4-A12	11.5-19	x	tr	x	tr	...	x	...	xx	...
R4-B2t	19-45.5	xx	tr	xx	x	...	xx	tr	xx	...
R4-Clox	45.5-57	...	...	tr	...	...	xx	tr	x	xx
R4-C2ox	57-67	...	...	tr	...	...	xxx	tr	xx	xxx
R4-Cn(1)	70	...	...	tr	...	...	tr	tr	xx	tr
R4-Cn(2)	85	tr	...	x	tr	...	xx	tr	x	xxx
R5-Ap	0-30.5	x	...	x	x	...	xx	tr	xx	...
R5-B2ir	30.5-58.5	tr	tr	xx	tr	...	xx	tr	xx	...
R5-Clox	58.5-84	tr	tr	x	tr	...	tr	tr	xx	x
R5-C2ox	84-109.5	tr	...	tr	tr	...	xxx	tr	x	xxx
R5-Cn(1)	122	...	...	tr	...	...	xxx	...	tr	xx
R5-Cn(2)	183	...	...	tr	...	...	xxx	tr	x	xxx
R9-Ap	0-23	tr	tr	tr	tr	...	x	tr	xx	...
R9-B2ir	23-53.5	x	tr	x	tr	...	xx	tr	x	x
R9-Cox	53.5-79	tr	...	xx	tr	...	xx	tr	x	xxx
R9-Cn	79+	tr?	...	tr	tr	...	xxx	tr	x	xxx

[a] Mineral abundance is based on peak height: minor amount (tr); small amount (x); medium amount (xx); abundant (xxx); ... no detection.

[b] Soil pits (e.g. R4, R9) can be located on Figs. 4 and 5.

Soil Chemistry

The soil pH ranges from 7.7 to 8.0 in the surface horizons, increasing to 8.4-8.6 in the subsurface horizons (Table 4.5). This trend is paralleled by a decrease in H^+ ion activity with depth, from nearly 3.0 (meq/100 g) in the surface to 0.6-0.1 meq/100 g in the parent material. The mobile cations Na^+ and Ca^{+2} tend to be more highly dispersed throughout these profiles when compared with natural soils. K^+ tends to dominate in horizons with higher amounts of illite, and Mg^{+2} dominates in the solum where chlorite tends to form.

The CEC, while not as high as in soils under forest cover, is highest in the solum. Calcium carbonate is slightly higher in the surface horizons as a function of fertilizer application. The percent base saturation is constant at 100, and salts are similar to the distribution reported in Chapters 2 and 3. Organic matter is significantly lower than in profiles under forest and grass cover (e.g. 2.4-3.0% in A horizons). A horizons have one-quarter the organic matter, and one-third the organic carbon of forest and grassland soils. Similarly nitrogen is at one-half the average value in forest soils, and the typical C:N ratio of 13:1 is somewhat lower than in soils under forest cover.

Phosphorus does not show any significant differences as a result of agricultural practices, and Fe_2O_3 is fairly evenly distributed between sites. Moisture retention is also similar to soils in forested and grassland areas.

Pesticides

DDT is lower in most sites affected by tillage, and it is generally absent in surface horizons. An exception to this is site R9 where p,p' DDT reaches 0.45 ppm in the A horizon. The presence of DDT and DDE at depth in site R4 is either a function of ground water influx and/or leaching. Atrazine, a common herbicide, is in the surface horizons of all profiles. The higher retention of pesticides in profile R9 is explained by the fine texture and higher adsorption of the lacustrine sediments.

Conclusions

Soils in plowed fields appear to have been affected by

Table 4.5. Selected chemical properties of the <2mm fractions of the horizons in Table 4.1.

Sample [a]	Depth (cm)	Exchangeable Cations (meq/100g)						CEC meq/100g	$CaCO_3$ %	Base Sat. %	Salts mmhos/cm	O.M. %	O.C. %	N %	C:N	P ppm 1:20 $NaHCO_3$	Fe_2O_3 %	Oven Dried Moisture %
		pH	H+	K+	Ca++	Mg++	Na+											
Site Horizon																		
R3-Ap	0-28	8.0	2.5	0.26	37.0	0.53	0.17	12.16	1.9	100	1.00	2.96	1.72	0.13	13:1	24.33	1.12	1.56
R3-B2ir	28-40.5	8.2	3.0	0.15	37.0	0.46	0.04	10.26	2.2	100	0.51	1.20	0.70	0.06	12:1	4.41	1.92	1.52
R3-Cox	40.5-63.5	8.6	0.4	0.05	37.0	0.43	0.04	1.66	19.1	100	0.44	0.23	0.13	0.01	13:1	1.31	0.55	0.34
R3-Cn	63.5+	8.4	0.1	0.02	35.0	0.43	tr	1.43	19.8	100	0.45	0.23	0.13	0.01	13:1	1.96	0.46	0.30
R4-A11	0-11.5	7.7	2.3	0.12	14.1	0.36	0.10	11.5	0.2	100	0.39	2.88	1.67	0.11	15:1	18.13	2.03	1.32
R4-A12	11.5-19	8.1	2.1	0.11	15.9	0.36	0.10	10.8	0.3	100	0.35	2.26	1.31	0.11	12:1	3.43	1.92	1.30
R4-B2t	19-45.5	8.1	2.1	0.15	23.0	0.46	0.13	10.9	0.5	100	0.33	0.85	0.49	0.05	10:1	4.08	2.83	1.65
R4-C1ox	45.5-57	8.5	1.1	0.04	27.0	0.30	0.10	2.3	14.0	100	0.40	0.34	0.20	0.01	20:1	2.78	0.70	0.48
R4-C2ox	57-67	8.5	0.3	0.04	29.0	0.43	0.09	1.6	18.8	100	0.35	0.23	0.13	0.01	13:1	0.98	0.84	0.36
R4-Cn(1)	70	8.5	0.6	0.02	25.0	0.36	0.09	1.1	17.5	100	0.30	0.17	0.10	tr	10:1	2.45	0.36	0.14
R4-Cn(2)	85	8.5	0.6	0.07	29.0	0.53	0.09	2.3	18.1	100	0.45	0.11	0.06	tr	6:1	3.27	0.78	0.42
R5-Ap	0-30.5	8.1	2.8	0.16	37.0	0.59	0.09	9.64	2.4	100	0.62	2.41	1.40	0.11	13:1	5.10	1.36	1.32
R5-B2ir	30.5-58.5	8.3	2.1	0.15	42.0	0.59	0.09	8.84	5.7	100	0.38	0.62	0.36	0.05	7:1	3.43	1.47	1.42
R5-C1ox	58.5-84	8.3	2.0	0.19	38.0	0.53	0.21	7.55	6.0	100	0.49	0.67	0.39	0.04	10:1	2.94	1.58	1.34
R5-C2ox	84-109.5	8.2	0.3	0.11	38.0	0.46	0.09	4.32	14.6	100	0.52	0.39	0.23	0.02	12:1	1.47	0.92	0.74
R5-Cn(1)	122	8.5	0.1	0.11	38.0	1.1	0.02	2.76	21.2	100	0.41	0.11	0.06	0.01	6:1	0.98	0.58	0.54
R5-Cn(2)	183	8.6	0.1	0.09	38.0	0.76	tr	2.71	16.6	100	0.36	0.11	0.06	0.01	6:1	1.80	0.66	0.52
R9-Ap	0-23	8.0	3.1	0.26	32.0	0.76	0.07	12.54	1.0	100	1.21	2.79	1.62	0.14	12:1	24.50	1.19	1.52
R9-B2ir	23-53.5	8.3	2.1	0.22	43.0	0.92	0.09	11.40	9.6	100	0.39	1.14	0.66	0.06	11:1	0.80	1.70	1.79
R9-Cox	53.5-79	8.6	0.9	0.18	40.0	1.3	0.09	7.89	23.7	100	0.39	0.51	0.30	0.03	10:1	2.45	0.97	1.30
R9-Cn	79+	8.4	0.8	0.18	42.0	2.3	0.09	8.03	23.6	100	0.48	0.29	0.17	0.02	9:1	1.96	0.86	1.34

[a] Soil pits (e.g. R4, R9) can be located on Figs. 4 and 5.

Table 4.6. Pesticide concentration for the horizons in Table 4.1.

Sample[a]	Depth (cm)	<2mm fractions (ppm)					
		p,p' DDT	o,p' DDT	DDE	DDD	Dieldrin	Atrazine
Site Horizon							
R3-Ap	0-28	...	...	...	...	...	0.07
R3-B2ir	28-40.5	...	...	...	...	...	.004
R3-Cox	40.5-63.5	...	...	...	...	...	.003
R3-Cn	63.5+	...	...	...	...	...	.005
R4-A11	0-11.5	...	...	...	...	...	0.03
R4-A12	11.5-19	...	...	...	...	...	0.02
R4-B2t	19-45.5	...	...	...	...	...	...
R4-Clox	45.5-57	...	...	...	...	...	...
R4-C2ox	57-67	...	...	...	...	...	...
R4-Cn(1)	70	...	...	...	...	...	...
R4-Cn(2)	85	.002	...	.001	tr	...	...
R5-Ap	0-30.5	.001	...	tr	...	...	0.01
R5-B2ir	30.5-58.5	...	...	...	...	...	.005
R5-Clox	58.5-84	...	...	...	...	...	...
R5-C2ox	84-109.5	...	...	...	...	...	...
R5-Cn(1)	122	...	...	...	...	...	...
R5-Cn(2)	183	...	...	...	...	...	...
R9-Ap	0-23	0.45	.063	0.34	tr	.003	0.05
R9-B2ir	23-53.5	...	...	...	...	...	0.01
R9-Cox	53.5-79	...	...	...	...	...	.005
R9-Cn	79+	...	...	...	...	...	.004

a ... no detection. Soil pits (e.g. R4, R9) can be located on Figs. 4 and 5.

agriculture in a number of important ways. Plowing induces
changes in the solum (A and B horizons) such that O horizons
are destroyed, and A and B horizons appreciably modified.
Horizons are generally thinner than in forest soils, and
the usual granular structure, so prevalent and well developed
in the forest soils, is destroyed. Fallow sites regain a
well-aerated granular structure in less than a decade, but
humus depletion, as a result of agriculture, is longer-lived
requiring greater time to restore organic matter.

The particle-size data indicate that clay is higher
in the solum of plowed horizons than in forest soils. This
suggests that abrasion as a result of plowing leads to a
reduction in size and production of material of clay size
($<4\mu$). Generally, the absence of silt in surface horizons
indicates that wind erosion in open fields needs additional
research.

The weathering sequence of illite-montmorillonite >
illite > montmorillonite > kaolin minerals is similar to the
sequence for forest soils. With respect to the soil chemistry,
total cation exchange capacity, organic matter, organic carbon, and nitrogen are significantly lower in plowed horizons.
Pesticides, including o,p' DDT, p,p' DDT, DDE and atrazine,
are found in all profiles. Patterns of pesticide dispersal
indicate that leaching and groundwater fluctuation play an
important role in the translocation of toxic substances.

The overall pattern of the data indicate that important
changes occur in the soil system as a result of agricultural
practices. These suggest that future work is needed in the
following areas:

(1) To analyze the geobiochemical changes that occur
in soil systems from termination of plowing to
full recovery of original profile characteristics
under fallow conditions.

(2) To determine the rate at which silt (e.g. 63-4μ)
size particles are removed from the surface of
plowed fields.

(3) To analyze the relationships between individual
clay minerals and common pesticides such as
DDT, and to determine residence time of pesticides in podzolic profiles under controlled
conditions.

111

CHAPTER 5

PERSPECTIVE ON AGRICULTURE AND URBANIZATION

Since urbanization is rapidly consuming the 7 million hectares of agricultural land in Ontario, it is important to study the effects of human activity on the natural environment. The technical analyses in the previous chapters clearly demonstrate the physical and geobiochemical character of the natural environment, and suggest the physical and biochemical changes which occur as a result of plowing, fertilizer and pesticide application. This chapter seeks to provide a general, descriptive perspective of the human impact on the natural environment in the study area, attempts to elucidate the historical context, and supplement the technical assessment.

Urbanization is here simply defined as the processes involving the transformation of agricultural lands for non-agrarian purposes. It is thus not solely restricted to the large scale irreversible conversions to residential uses that are typically found at the periphery of major metropolitan areas. Because, in the study area, urban growth is concentrated and generally limited to the extreme southern sections which are continuous to Toronto. Instead, this chapter focusses concisely on the settlement history of the study area as it is relevant to land utilization. It describes the early Indian settlements and their limited impact on the environment through their semi-sedentary agriculture. The chapter proceeds to discuss the timing of European settlement, associated problems such as transportation and the external economic context and the agricultural practices of the settlers. The final section discusses the growth of urban settlements, their service functions, their limited industrial base and their economic stagnation. It also traces trends of land use changes and lists some of the reasons why the study area, in spite of its proximity to Toronto, never realized its potential for urbanization.

Indian Settlement and Agriculture

The earliest evidence of Indian occupation found in the study area dates from about 5,000 years BP (Konrad and Ross, 1974, p. 19). The Indian occupancy of the land was, however, not continuous. In reconstructing the process of

113

Indian settlement, Konrad and Ross (1974, p. 21) used archaeological evidence and known radiocarbon dates to hypothesize
that the area was twice abandoned by Indians prior to the
arrival of European settlers. It was first abandoned for
unknown reasons around 3,000 years BP. This "Archaic" Indian
culture congregated in villages in the summer, dispersing
in the winter in order to find food through hunting and
gathering (Greewald, 1973, p. 4). By about 1,000 years BP
the Iroquois moved into the study area, only to abandon it
during the Iroquois-Huron wars in the 17th century (Bowman,
1974, p. 17). Bowman (1974) provides supporting evidence
for this hypothesis in the form of fossil pollen records
found in Lake Ontario which indicate that a few of the prime
stands in the area that were found by the first European
settlers must have been a colonization of once cleared areas.

When the Indians returned to the area approximately
1,000 years ago they were not hunters and gatherers but, in-
deed, incipient agriculturalists, practicing shifting cultivation (Jones, 1964, p. 8; Konrad and Ross, 1974, p. 25).
The Indian encampments tended to be near sources of water
but were neither individually extensive nor did they result
in large clearings in the area. The size of the fields they
would cultivate at one time was limited to a 'safe distance'
which they could defend easily (Heidenreich, 1972, p. 67).

The Indians located their villages, and therefore
their cultivated clearings, on sandy loam and loam soils.
These tended to be well-drained locations, therefore freer
from insects, and furthermore, they would dry out earlier
in spring affording a longer growing period (Konrad and Ross,
1974). They avoided clay areas, no doubt, for the additional
reason that their rudimentary implements would have posed
severe problems for cultivation. Their use of the slash
and burn technique of clearing the forest cover brought them
sustained yields for long periods of time, because the ashes
were rich in calcium, magnesium, potassium and phosphorous
and had the effect of increasing soil fertility (Heidenreich,
1972).

When the fields lost their fertility the whole en-
campment would move, generally only a few miles in order to
farm new land and to locate a new source of firewood. This
settlement process explains the dense concentration of
village sites in sections of the study area although the
sites were not all occupied at the same time (Greenwald,
1973, p. 6-10; Konrad and Ross, 1974, p. 18).

In contrast to the European agriculturalists who came later, the Indians were more attuned to the compatibility of their needs with the surrounding forests, and therefore they did not cultivate large fields. Their simple hoe and digging-stick form of agriculture may not have favored high crop yields but it meant only a shallow upturning of the soil which conserved moisture and organic matter (see Chapter 4 which contains the analysis of the effect of plowing on soil organic matter and humus). Corn, one of the staple foods of the Indians, was grown in the fields near their settlements. But, they also grew beans and squash, and had an almost wholly vegetarian diet (Konrad and Ross, 1974, p. 26).

When the first Europeans entered the study area there remained only one Seneca Indian village, Ganetsekwyagon (Mitchell, 1950). The Hurons had moved north to the area around Georgian Bay and Lake Simcoe. The Iroquois had moved substantially further east and south (Bonis, 1956, pp. 26-29). Thus, when European settlement began it was virtually virgin forest that confronted the Europeans (Mitchell, 1950). Since the study area lies within the deciduous forest region of Canada (Rowe, 1972) the pioneers encountered land that was occupied by a climax vegetation consisting of primarily sugar maple and beech, together with basswood, red maple, red oak, white oak, and burr oak (for details of forest cover types see Chapter 1). This climax vegetation covered the land from Oshawa to Sarnia and to Niagara. It had reestablished itself even on the lands abandoned after Indian occupancy.

European Settlement

While French missionaries had traversed the study area in the 17th century (Bonis, 1965), and there had been a French fort, Fort Rouille, in the Toronto region in the early 18th century (Mitchell, 1950), settlement did not officially begin until Lord Dorchester, Captain General of the Province of Quebec, divided the Province first into a number of districts, in 1788; then, in 1791, into Upper Canada and Lower Canada, and in 1792 he established the counties, including York and Ontario. The surveying of the townships was accomplished by Augustus Jones between 1791 and 1795 (Wood, 1911; Bonis, 1965).

While Scarborough and Pickering townships were surveyed first, because they were adjacent to the newly chosen capital, York (Toronto), Markham township was the first to

115

have settlers (Greenwald, 1973, p. 21). Land was cheap and
the Crown usually alloted it in 80 hectare (200 acre) blocks.
Military men and 'United Empire Loyalists' were given the
land free, whereas settlers purchased it at about two dollars
per acre. The early settlers along the Rouge River were
largely German Lutherans from New York, Berczy Germans, and
Pennsylvania Germans. The settlers were given a 'location
ticket' to settle a particular parcel of land, and had to
fulfill two major settlement duties before the Crown granted
them patents for the land. Settlers had to clear a strip
of land 50 m (165 feet) wide along the lot's frontage, and
clear a total of 12 hectares (30 acres). Since most of the
land was covered by bush much clearing had to be done before
the settlers could farm the land. The clearings which sur-
rounded the log dwellings of the settlers were used almost
entirely to support the family who farmed them. But, according to Wood (1911, p. 181), the settlers early gave
their attention to the effective cultivation of soil and
the furnishing of their farms with stock of good quality.
While these settlement duties were the beginning of the movement to clear the land of the orginal forest cover there was,
generally, a substantial timelag between the settling of the
land and the taking out of a patent.

Transportation was a problem that plagued the study
area for decades and had a profound impact on the timing of
settlement and severely constrained the distribution of
goods. At first the settlers used old Indian trails. These
and the early roads they opened to riverside mills, more
accurately described as paths blazed into the primeval forest,
followed the topography. While the settlement of Markham
flourished early because of the existence of Yonge Street
to Toronto, the settlement of Scarborough and Pickering was
delayed partially because of the absence of a good road,
since the Kingston road, opened in 1799, was of poor quality
until after the war of 1812 (Greenwald, 1973, p. 25). The
grid survey pattern was used to plan road allowances, and
later, settlement began to link-up along the grid road system
(Richardson, 1956). However, the process of building an
easily traveled road took decades.

Another major influence on the timing of settlement
was,paradoxically, that it was nearly impossible to find
vacant crown land by the 1810's, yet most of the land remained uncleared until the 1820's and 1830's (Wood, 1911).
Speculators held much of the land and did not break up their
holdings in the early days in order to increase demand for
land and, hence, increase the price of lots (Greenwald, 1973,

p. 25). While the early settlers were mostly American, after 1816 British immigrants arrived in larger numbers. In 1825 just under 13 thousand immigrants came up the St. Lawrence, beginning a 15-year migration that was to clear and fence York county (Mitchell, 1950, p. 60). The timber was a resource as well as a hindrance; in addition to the clearances for patenting the land, trees were felled to build the house and the barn, to clear land for crops and the settlers continued to clear the land selling the wood to the railways and steamboats and often did not even leave shade trees (Jones, 1946). Moreover, burning the hardwood timber produced potash as an early cash crop. Yet it is recorded that it was not until 1851 that over 50 percent of Pickering township (Ontario county) had been cleared of trees. But the 'assault' on the rest of the forest was being accelerated every year (Wood, 1911, p. 107).

The external economic situation also had a profound influence on the timing of settlement and the vitality and economic stability of agriculture and trade in the study area. For example, with the changes in the 'Corn Laws' in Great Britain in the 1820's which lowered, and finally removed, the tariff on imported grains, wheat farming became an important activity from the 1830's to the 1860's (Jones, 1946). The wheat was exported to the United States and England. Wheat growing reassured farmers that their future looked prosperous. Its effects could be seen in the bigger and better barns required for this type of farming, the clearing of extra land that it encouraged, and the fine red brick houses of the 1850's and 1860's (Greenwald, 1973, p. 33). More specifically, the 1851 Census of Pickering reflects this prosperity. Of the 24,503 hectares (61,258 acres) held by families, 9,008 hectares (22,520 acres) were under tillage, 3,125 hectares (7,813 acres) under pasture, 12,332 hectares (30,830 acres) were under forest cover, but only 38 hectares (95 acres) were considered unfit for cultivation. Some of the products listed were wheat, barley, rye, oats, Indian corn, potatoes, butter, cheese, flax, wool and maple sugar. Lumbering also increased in importance and many saw mills provided the settlers with construction lumber.

The market for Ontario wheat collapsed by the 1860's substantially because the American Midwest took over the market (Jones, 1946, p. 196). The opening of the Canadian Prairies in the 1880's and the ability of railway transportation to bring cheaper high-class wheat into Ontario perpetuated the steady decline in the acreages devoted to wheat in Ontario. Farmers had to diversify their farming. Because of reciprocity treaties with the United States barley had become an important export crop by the 1860's. It was largely grown for breweries in the United States until the 1880's (Jones, 1946, p. 242). The diversification of agriculture ameliorated only partially the effects of the depression of the mid 1870's, the recession in the 1880's and the depression in the following decade. As farm commodity prices and production fell many famers began selling their remaining woodlots for lumber to supplement farm incomes (see Table 1.2). Whereas in the 1830's the primeval forest was just a few hundred meters from the survey concession line and the occasional pioneer cabin, by the late 1880's there remained virtually no high quality agricultural land to be cleared in the study area. In fact the farmers were so thorough in their clearing of the climax vegetation that had existed for thousands of years that now many had to buy cordwood for their own use (Jones, 1946).

Agricultural Practices

While the early Ontario settlers saw the forest cover on the land as a hindrance, it was nevertheless a useful means of gauging the quality of the soil under the forest. When the surveyors were dispatched between 1791 and 1795 to mark-out the land, they were expressly instructed to take note of the ground cover, and to base an elementary classification of the soils by the types of trees found growing on them. "When a man perceives that walnut, chestnut, hickory, basswood and maple are promiscuously scattered over his estate, he need not be at all apprehensive of having to cultivate an unproductive soil" (Jones, 1946, p. 20). In addition, Albrecht (1971, p. 399) explains how the pioneer farmers would take a handful of soil and let it run through their fingers in order to assess the granular structure of the soil. Its presence in the soil horizon indicated the degree of fertility.

The settlers knew that the plant life above the soil and soil fertility are inextricably interwoven via a simple and attestable process: plants grow on, and are supported by the soil. They derive the nutrients they require to grow from the soil itself. When plants die they decay on the ground, allowing microorganisms in the soil to attack the plants and in the decay process to return nutrients to the soil for further plant life and thereby completion of the cycle.

The removal of the forest cover in Ontario was accomplished through a simple method. Whether land was
cleared for agriculture or lumber was needed to build the
homestead, the settlers would cut the trees but leave the
stumps in the ground. Jones (1946) discusses the difficulties
the early setters must have had. They would clear one and
one-half to two hectares (four or five acres) and sow their
first crop probably corn. The clearing would be cultivated
with just a hoe and harrow and the stumps remaining in the
ground were, no doubt, a constant source of annoyance. The
following year the settlers would clear another one and one-
half to two hectares and again cultivate corn. The older
clearings were left in hay or pasture; or perhaps oats or
rye. After four or five years the roots of the stumps would
have decayed enough to permit the use of a plow. Even then
the settlers, generally, did not remove all the stumps but
would keep running the plow around the stumps until the soil
moved.

Crop rotation was commonly used in the study area in
the 1850's to prolong the fertility and usefulness of the
soil. The settlers knew that certain plants did not just
remove nutrients from the soil but that they contributed
nutrients to the medium as well. And these plants, usually
legumes, if grown in rotation with cereals help sustain
yields for longer time periods. Crop rotation as used by
farmers in England, was adopted from the Dutch early in the
17th century (Dale and Carter, 1955), and presumably was
the same idea that was brought with the first American and
British settlers to Canada. How widespread the use of these
farming techniques was may be ascertained by the existence
of local agricultural societies, (founded as early as 1844
in Scarborough, 1850 in Pickering and 1855 in Markham) whose
aim it was to discuss and propagate good techniques and crop
rotations (Jones, 1946, p. 168).

However, prior to 1850 one of the most significant
aspects of early farming in the study area was the use of
'naked summer fallow' (Jones, 1946, p. 91). Unfortunately,
it was a naked fallow plowed crosswise and lengthwise and
harrowed between the plowings. This meant that the fields
were plowed across the contours. Not only did an extensive
mixing of the soil horizons occur but, in addition, the soil
was left naked. As the study area comprises rolling country-
side this method is almost certain to have provided ready-
made channels for concentrated overland flow, and sheet
erosion after rainstorms (see Chapter 4 for analytical

119

findings)[a]. Fortunately, summer fallow was abandoned, not because any environmental danger was seen in it, but because it was considered wasteful not to utilize the fields (Jones, 1946, p. 92). Up to about 1850, the farmers used a long eight to ten year rotation of peas, fallow, wheat, grain, wheat and then for four or five years fallow. By this time Indian corn was no longer farmed because of the frost risk as well as the drudgery of hoeing. Wheat was the important cash crop. By the 1860's barley had replaced fall wheat in the study area (Jones, 1946, p. 247). Where spring wheat or barley was grown the summer fallow had disappeared.

In order to maintain and improve the soil some form of fertilizer was used. While bone and mineral superphosphate fertilizers were available few farmers could afford them (Jones, 1946, p. 325). Therefore, with the increase in livestock-rearing manure was the ubiquitous fertilizer.

Mechanization had been brought to agriculture by McCormick and Hussey's reaping machine at the beginning of the 19th century but mechanization did not have a large impact on the study area until threshing machines were introduced into Upper Canada from New York in the 1830's. By 1843, threshing machines had come into general use throughout the wheat growing sections of Upper Canada (Jones, 1946). Continual improvements were also made in such agricultural implements as the narrow and the deep-delving wheeled plow (Jones, 1946, p. 91). The improved plows helped sustain yields but with continued usage had a negative effect on the soil (see findings of Chapter 4).

While crop rotation was a useful means to preserve the fertility of the soil in the study area until the late 1940's, farmers of today rely on chemical and mineral fertilizers to increase yields and output per hectare and on chemical pesticides to guard against insects or other pests. As in other parts of Ontario a major practice is the liming of soil, originally to remove soil acidity, in order to restock it with calcium and magnesium. These elements are essential in active amounts within the soil for exchange to

---

[a]Butzer (1974, p. 64) notes that appreciable sheet erosion occurs on slopes with an angle as small as two degrees, and that rill erosion occurs on slopes of five degrees. He estimates that the theoretical time necessary to erode 175 mm of soil on bare ground fallow is only 17 years, as opposed to 173,700 years under forest cover.

the plant roots. Phosphorous is also used both as the natural mineral and in the chemically treated form. Other chemical elements, like potassium, serve in smaller active amounts in the soil and are required as treatment if soils are to produce.

Unfortunately, the use of chemical fertilizers in the study area, over a long period of time, has led to a deterioration of the organic structure of the soil (see Chapter 4). Farmers in the area estimated, during personal interviews, that without fertilization and under continuous cropping, they would only expect to get crops for four years.

In conclusion, at the beginning of European settlement the study area was basically an agricultural region of subsistence farming. The farmers were self-reliant, learning how to use the many materials found on the land. But, soon there were the first tangible signs of progress from subsistence farming to commercial farming, which became the primary support of the economy (Careless, 1967, p. 29). The continuous indiscriminate cropping of wheat lead to the exhaustion of the soil, and the collapse of the market for Ontario wheat in the 1860's led to a diversification of agriculture. During the agricultural depressions of the late 19th century the pattern that became firmly set during the 20th century began to evolve: mixed farming with dairying and stock raising, a small farm population and an increased reliance on technology.

Urbanization and Land Use

The growth of urban settlements in the study area was fostered by the farmers' increasing prosperity between the 1820's and 1850's, as a result of the lucrative export trade of wheat, and their increasing demand for a wider variety of goods and services. Several small service centers, such as Markham, Cedar Grove, Cherrywood and others, were distributed in a regular pattern throughout the study area. During this time life evolved into a routine, centered on the cyclical life of the farm, the interdependence of the farmers with their villages and linkages of these small urban settlements with the rest of Ontario (Greenwald, 1973, p. 49).

Closely related to urbanization and population growth in the 1850's and 1860's was the establishment of a limited industrial base for the urban settlements; generally, saw mills, grist mills and, eventually, woollen mills (Gentilcore, 1963, p. 78). On West Duffin's Creek there were at one time no less than twenty water powered mills (Greenwald, 1973, p. 33). Sometimes, the mills formed the nucleus of new urban settlements, for instance Cedar Grove. The mills also often acted as catalysts for the creation of ancillary industries. For example, the existence of a saw mill and sash factory. In this way each urban place in the study area developed its own, limited, industrial base. Clearly these 'industries' were not large, employing perhaps between five and ten persons, depending on the season. Those factories powered by water made use of the spring runoff to produce their products (Greenwald, 1973, p. 73). It was not until technological changes required larger and more complicated industries, and railway transportation came to the study area in the 1880's, that many mills and factories could no longer compete and were forced to close (Greenwald, 1973, p. 38-39).

The arrival of the railroad had a major impact on the urban settlements in the study area. The building of the 'Toronto and Nipissing' (now Canadian National) in 1872, the 'Ontario and Quebec' (now Canadian Pacific) in 1884, and the 'Campbellford, Lake Ontario and Western (now Canadian Pacific) in 1912, provided not only transportation for goods produced by the small village industries, but also gave farmers easy access to the growing urban markets of Toronto for their produce and for their supplies (Innis, 1971, p. 156; Stevens, 1962, p. 72). The proximity of Toronto encouraged dairy farming, the founding of the dairy industry, cheese factories and creameries, poultry raising and truck gardening (Richardson, 1956, p. 141). A station in the urban place attracted varying commercial activities such as warehouses, wholesalers, and grain elevators. The reliability, speed and relative ease of the railway expanded the urban settlement's limits. Now, not only was Toronto easily accessible but its economic and social influence on the study area increased substantially (Innis, 1971). This potential for urbanization in the study area was, however, never realized because of the agricultural depressions of the 1870's to 1890's. They led to farm abandonment and farm amalgamation, rural depopulation, and to the large-scale movement of people to the towns and cities elsewhere in Ontario, or westward to the newly opened Canadian Prairies. The small urban settlements stagnated economically and their population levels remained static for the next 50-60 years.

From 1900 until the mid 1950's while Toronto experienced substantial urban growth and developed into a metro-

politan urban region the study area, in spite of its proximity, substantially escaped urbanization and remained an
agricultural region. The size of the small urban settlements
had remained static and they still fulfilled their service
role for the agricultural hinterland. The effects of the
centrifugal urban growth generated in Toronto were substantially limited in the study area to land use changes
for two large hydro transmission right-of-ways which con-
verge on the Cherrywood transformer station; for transportation systems, such as five permanent railways and several
major highways; for quarries, for brick-making as well as
sand and gravel and later for sanitary land fills. Since
there was no serious shortage of housing in Toronto to create
an overspill-effect, demand for residential development was
stable, and generally limited to the natural increase of the
population in the study area. The reason for this was that
the main thrust of Toronto's dynamic urban growth was histori-
cally directed to the west. According to the Canada Census
of Population between 1961 and 1971 the annual net migration
into the Toronto Census Metropolitan Area was about 55,000
persons!

If land use is a measure of human activity then the
following description of changes in land use during the last
15 years is a general reflection of the spatial extent and
temporal progress of urbanization in the study area. Clearly,
a map showing the land area used for industry, housing and
other uses does not reveal the variations of land uses within
any category, the intensity of uses, the complexity of
mixtures of land uses within a single development nor the
effects of different uses on the environment. But, the
following maps document the magnitude of urbanization,
measured in terms of land use changes between 1958, 1966
and 1971 (see Figs. 5.1, 5.2, 5.3). A comparison of the
maps clearly shows several major trends. Firstly, the agriculturally productive lands have decreased everywhere but
the trend of land conversion to residential uses is most
pronounced in the southern section of the study area. This
area is contiguous to the urban concentration of the metropolis to the west and, consequently, absorbed the east-
ward growth thrust eminating from Toronto and exhibits the
most extensive effects of urbanization on the natural environment. Secondly, because of Toronto's dominance as an
employment and retail center, industrial land uses have
slightly decreased and commercial land uses have only margin-
ally increased. Thirdly, there is a steady and substantial
increase in the land areas devoted to 'open-space', especially
along the Highland Creek and Rouge River valleys, and

123

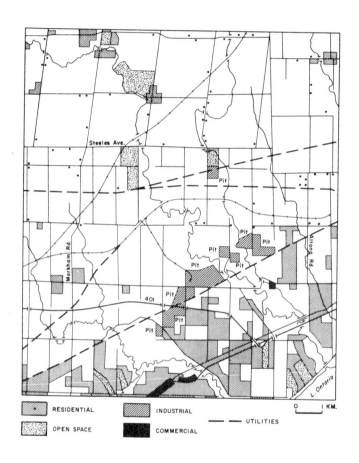

Figure 5.1. Land use, 1958 (Metropolitan Toronto
Planning Board, 1959).

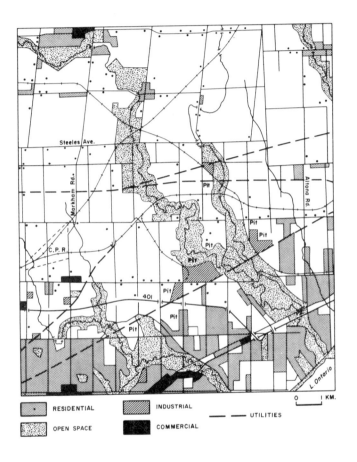

Figure 5.2.   Land use, 1966 (Metropolitan Toronto
              Planning Board, 1974).

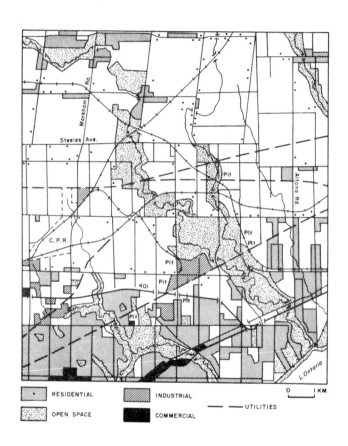

Figure 5.3.   Land use, 1971 (Metropolitan Toronto
              Planning Board, 1974).

126

including four formerly active open sand and gravel pits,
three of which are now occupied by the new Metropolitan
Toronto zoo. This was accomplished through land acquisition
policies by the Metropolitan Toronto and Region Conservation
Authority and the government of the Municipality of Metropolitan Toronto. The aim of these policies is to keep all
of the major valley lands free of urban development as part
of the overall flood control and conservation program (Metropolitan Toronto Planning Board, 1959, p. 232). Fourthly,
the study area proper, which contains the major soil sampling
sites (see Fig. 1.3) with the exception of rural non-farm
housing is still unaffected by urbanization in 1971 (see
Fig. 5.3).

Since 1971, however, the study area has been vulner-
able not only to the urban development policies of Metropolitan Toronto, but also to provincial economic planning
efforts and to the spill-over effects of massive federal
acquisition of 7,600 hectares of prime agricultural lands
immediately to the east, for the now cancelled New Toronto
International Airport.

The centripedal forces accounting for the proliferation of jobs, residences and retail establishments in the
urban core of Toronto have generated a centrifugal growth
component that seeks to draw continuous, non-urban lands
as well as local municipalities into the growth sphere of
Metropolitan Toronto. Pressures to expand services and
facilities in order to absorb centrifugal urban growth
generated in Toronto's core have placed serious strains on
the capability of the surrounding natural environment to
provide for all the necessary requisites of urban growth.
Consequently, based on the rationale that urban and economic
growth affects the entire region, encompassing several municipalities, the Ontario Government introduced an ambitious
scheme to direct the growth of Toronto and surrounding municipalities in a regional context (Bureau of Municipal
Research, 1974, p. 3). With the publication of Design for
Development: The Toronto Centred Region (Government of
Ontario, 1970), and its status report in 1971, (Government
of Ontario, 1971), the Provincial Government demonstrated
its intention to strengthen local government in the "Toronto
Centred Region" (TCR) through the creation of regional governments, and to relate this governmental restructuring to
Provincial economic development through the creation of five
planning regions (Government of Ontario, 1970). The regional
governments that compose the Central Ontario Lakeshore Urban
Complex (COLUC, 1974), which is the successor of the TCR,

within the larger Provincial Central Ontario Region are
Metropolitan Toronto (created in 1953), York (1971), Durham
(1974), Halton (1974), Peel (1974), and Hamilton-Wentworth
(1974). Under the Provincial "Planning Act" each regional
municipality is an independent planning area and each will
produce an official plan for the area of its jurisdiction.
However, the Province retains jurisdiction for overall regional planning strategies. The following discussion is
based on these broad Provincial regional planning strategies,
especially as they affect the study area. In 1970, the
Ontario Government adopted as policy an urban structure that
was based substantially on the results of the earlier regional transportation study (MTARTS, 1967). The TCR concept
was envisaged as a framework within which most public and
private decisions affecting the region could be coordinated.
Ontario would retain the efficiency of the private sector
while improving the quality of life (COLUC, 1974, p. 3).
Design for Development (Government of Ontario, 1971) listed
12 goals for the TCR region against which to consider the
"vital social implications" of growth. The following three
goals are of particular interest regarding the relationship
between man and the environment:

(1) 'To preserve the unique attributes of the regional landscape;'

(2) 'To minimize the urban use of productive agricultural land;' and

(3) 'To minimize the pollution of water and the
atmosphere'

(COLUC, 1974, p. 3).

The document also lists five development principles designed
to help achieve the goals:

(1) the principle of linearity

(2) the principle of functional efficiency

(3) the principle of decentralization

(4) the principle of space conservation, and

(5) the principle of natural resource conservation

(MTARTS, 1967)

The last two principles are particularly interesting. The
principle of space conservation stresses adequate open space
and recreational requirements, on a per capita basis, while
the principle of natural resource conservation stresses the
careful use of land, water and air. The TCR report (1970)
expresses concern about what it calls the 'aspects of un-
structured sprawl' and deplores the premature removal of land
from agricultural and recreational uses at a rate that substantially exceeds the requirements for urban and residential
development. Some of this it attributes to speculative and
other urban generated pressures, some to lot creation by
consent (Committee of Adjustment), and some of it is un-
doubtedly passing into large non-farm holdings, outside the
consent granting and subdivision processes, and thus, often,
simply becoming idle.

The Toronto Centred Region conceptual structure can
be categorized in terms of the following five major principles
(COLUC, 1974, p. 4):

(1)   'Urban development structured along the lake-
        shore minimizes both water supply and sewage
        treatment costs and negative environmental
        effects.'

(2)   'A linear development exploits the efficiencies
        of high-capacity transportation facilities,
        particularly mass transit.'

(3)   'A second tier of urbanization separated from
        the lakeshore tier by a linear parkway belt
        system reduces congestion in the lakeshore tier
        and provides open space relief in the urban
        fabric, while the parkway belt houses transpor-
        tation and other utilities.'

(4)   'A range of city sizes forming a hierarchy
        provides diversity of living and working op-
        portunities, and brings services nearer to the
        consumer.'

(5)   'Development to the east, emphasized at the
        expense of growth in other parts of the area,
        flanks Toronto on both sides by structurally
        comparable sub-regions, thus achieving balance
        of opportunity, maximum personal access, and
        restraining congestion in the west.'

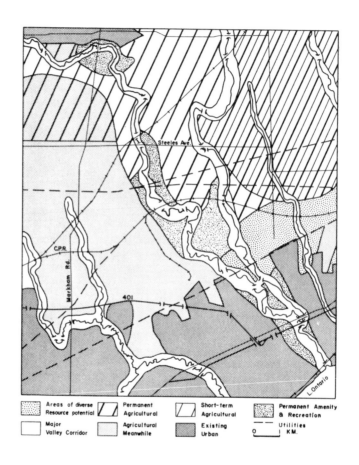

Figure 5.4. Future regional land use development
strategy (COLUC, 1974).

While the TCR concept was intended to provide guide-
lines and a policy framework it failed on several major
occasions, to some extent, because of the overly general
nature of the document which was insufficiently detailed to
give clear guidance to Provincial ministries. The Provincial
Regional Planning Branch responded to requests for clari-
fication in an _ad hoc_ fashion which was not only inconsistent
with sound planning but sometimes ran counter to the adopted
planning goals and principles. As a result an Advisory
Committee on Urban and Regional Planning was set up by the
Province in 1973 to refine the Toronto-Centred Region concept, now renamed Central Ontario Lakeshore Urban Complex
(COLUC), so that it can be used as a common framework by the
regional municipalities and the various agencies of the
Provincial government in formulating their policies and pro-
grams (COLUC, 1974). Fig. 5.4 shows the proposed future regional land use development strategy for the study area
according to the COLUC document.[1] The five previously discussed principles can be readily identified. The lands reserved for 'permanent amenity and recreation' and 'permanent
agriculture' virtually bisect the map and separate the two
tiers of urbanization. Virtually the only evidence of the
Provincial stimulation of urban growth east of Toronto is
the "Pickering New Town," part of which is located in the
northeastern section of the study area (Fig. 5.4). The most
recent Provincial land use plan for the proposed 6,800
hectare development states that about 4,160 hectares of rural
land will be preserved for farming, recreation, and parkland.
The New Town is expected to have a population of 75,000 by
1991, and will consist of 2,720 hectares of urban development,
with an average housing density of 32 units/hectare; about
31,500 jobs should be provided and about 440 hectares set
aside for industrial development. A recent study commissioned
by the City of Toronto (City of Toronto Planning Board, 1974)
regarding the impact of the New Town points out quite em-
phatically that the project may violate the goals and principles of COLUC (1974, p. 3),

> This notion of balanced or even growth is articulated
> only in terms of gross population and employment
> distribution. It pays no regard to the better use
> of the environment...It disregards the potentials of
> existing serviced land that have not yet been
> developed within municipal boundaries; it ignores

---

[1]. This document has not, as yet, been adopted as Provincial
policy.

recreational and environmental needs; and it gives
insufficient consideration to transportation con-
sequences of the nature and places of employment.

More specifically the study argues that people and
jobs would be spread more thinly over a yet wider area than
is presently true in the urbanized lake oriented corridor.
Instead of forming a dense, self-sufficient urban entity
that would look to Oshawa for higher-order goods and services,
it is feared that Toronto, and especially Scarborough, would
become very attractive (and accessible) for shopping and
entertainment functions. Such an orientation would, in time,
seek to consolidate the region from Toronto to the Pickering
New Town (and including the study area) into a single urban
metropolis.

The environmental impact of the direct urban pressures
and their shadow effects on the study area includes the agricultural land losses to the Province for the New Town project
in North Pickering. Unfortunately, no specific data are
available on the magnitude of agricultural land losses, due
to land severances for rural housing lots, and for assembly
by developers or speculators in the study area. Farmers re-
spond to the urban generated pressures in a number of different ways. Many are simply abandoning agriculture or winding
down their operations and retain farmland with the prospect
of sale. Others are selling off whole farms to developers
and to urban people seeking a country home. The latter
fragments the ownership pattern, often to the detriment of
farm operators. In addition, rural residential development
not only withdraws land from agriculture but also brings
servicing diseconomies, although the true picture of the
costs and benefits has not been tallied (Regional Municipality of York, 1972). The temptation to sell land out of agriculture is reinforced by the generally low returns available
in the farm economy and, especially, by the present approach
to taxation and assessment in Ontario which provides a built-
in development incentive. Farmland that has a higher value
due to development potential for urban and non-farm rural
uses is being taxed at a rate higher than its value in farm
use. The costs of hard and soft municipal services not required by farmers tend to be passed on to them anyway. Finally, many farmers in the study area are adjusting to the high
land-factor prices through intensification of non-land in-
puts as an alternative to expanding their enterprises or
turn to inherently intensive kinds of operation that enjoy
a comparative advantage from proximity to Toronto. Census
data, during the 1966-1971 period, confirms the existence of

intensification in the northern section of the study area. Intensification seems a sensible economic adjustment but it is giving rise to severe environmental impacts and nuisance effects which society may come to regard as intolerable.

CHAPTER 6

SUMMARY

Cultivation results in a thorough modification of
podzolic soils, and produces the plowed horizon (Ap). Turning
of the slice to a depth of ∼30 cm mixes soil material from
different genetic horizons and produces a tillage horizon of
uniform properties, differing from the properties and horizons of natural soil from which it is formed. Major changes
in morphology, moisture regime, and in the composition of
the organic and chemical profiles result from machine tillage
which induces considerable changes in the surface soil horizons. The data indicate that properties of agricultural
soils resulting from machine tillage are preserved for a long
time. Pesticides and fertilizers applied to the soil systems
dissipate quickly through the system, but trace quantities
remain behind in surface and subsurface horizons.

Podzolic soils forming in a forest environment have
properties reflecting the degree of soil development. At
the soil surface there is a thin, dark-colored zone of organic
matter accumulation (O1), underlain by a dark-colored humus-
rich horizon (A1). Below this zone some profiles have a
white-colored, eluvial horizon, low in humus and bases (A2).
In the lower solum there is an illuvial B horizon which in-
corporates weathering products leached from the upper solum,
including mobile compounds of iron which give a reddish-brown
color. Thickness and properties of genetic horizons vary
according to the degree of podzolization. Soil properties
change throughout the genetic horizons and a number of sub-
ordinate horizons may be distinguished as: O1, O2, A11,
A12, A1, A2, B1, B2t, B2ir, B3. Horizon boundaries are
sharpest in the upper accumulation horizons. Here the soil
is consistently penetrated by plant rootlets and soil fauna,
which slowly develop a granular or crumb structure, and concentration of humic colloids and organic matter in various
stages of decomposition and mineralization. Soil structure
governs the ease with which roots can penetrate the soil
medium and adsorb nutrients. The arrangement of particles
and voids influence the movement of soil solutions and gases,
and determine, to some extent, the fertility of soil. Tillage increases soil compaction, creates a massive structure,
overall higher bulk density, and shear-strength. As a result
of this mechanical stability is increased somewhat, while
root activity and development are curtailed.

135

The surface A horizons of forest soils have a stable structure, larger pore space, and numerous plant root structures which lead to a degree of permeability that differs from the lower A horizon complex. These horizons have lighter hues and lower humus, weaker granular structure, and display evidence of leaching. Beneath the A horizon complex, the B horizon constitutes a zone where illuviation of free iron oxides accumulate. The material of this horizon is compacted and dominated by weak blocky structural development, depending on the intensity of podzolization and texture. The underlying C horizons generally lack structural development and show overall lower humus content and higher shear-strength.

In soils subjected to plowing, not only the surface eluvial A horizon is plowed, but also the underlying B illuvial horizon. Plowing leads to intermixing of the genetic humus-accumulation horizons, the genetic horizons A11, A12, A1, A2, etc. are all destroyed and the Ap horizon is formed. Properties of the Ap horizon are determined by the nature of the materials in the genetic surface humus-accumulation horizons. The upper B horizons in plowed profiles are affected by turning of the slice and intermixing of materials. The decrease in overall pore space, as a result of plowing decreases the gas exchange between the soil and the atmosphere, and decreases overall porosity which is important for fertility and biogeochemical processes.

The increase in clay content as a result of tillage on forest soils is important as it affects the water holding capacity, porosity and permeability, and bulk density of the soil. Machine cultivation also affects the distribution of silt which is considerably lower in surface horizons. Reduction in particle size may result from machine tillage and partly from freeze-thaw as a result of the deeper penetration of the chill layer as discussed by Kachinskii (1927). Production of clay sized materials may even be greater than indicated here, as investigations by Low (1972) indicate that wind is a prime erosional agent of clay from clay loam soils in plowed fields in the U.K.

Clay mineralogy is similar in all the profiles studied showing little overall relationship to machine cultivation. The weathering sequence in plowed fields is quite similar to soils under forest cover. Soil systems influenced by shallow tillage and application of insecticides and herbicides display higher accumulation of clay in the surface, lower amounts of organic matter, and a lower carbon-nitrogen ratio.

136

Pesticide analyses suggest that DDT, DDD, DDE, dieldrin, and atrazine may be adsorbed by clay and humus colloids, but degrade quickly in plowed fields. On the other hand, soil chemistry is affected by machine cultivation and application of fertilizers and pesticides (Tables 4.5 and 4.6). Similar data are reported by Levin (1969) who analyzed a number of tilled soils in the U.S.S.R. As a result of the mechanical intermixing of organic material from the genetic horizons of forest soils, the Ap horizon contains a lower overall amount of organic materials.

Since urbanization is rapidly consuming the 7 million hectares of agricultural land in Ontario it is important to study the effects of agricultural activity on the natural environment. As this economic development continues, it is becoming increasingly difficult to locate, map and sample pristine, unaltered stands of mixed-hardwood forest. Moreover, changes in the character of the natural soil system as a result of plowing and pesticide application indicate that, as the total amount of arable land shrinks in size, more intensive forms of agriculture may further degrade existing cultivated soils.

RESUME

Le milieu naturel dans le centre du sud de l'Ontario est un
produit des glaciers Quarternary qui a déposé une moraine légère
sur la roche basse de l'âge Ordovician et Silurian; des sédiments
associés avec les époques entre les glaciers et les processus
postglacials. On peut analyser les régions des forêts caduques -
mixtes près de l'est de Toronto et dans les villes de Markham
et de Pickering et ramasser les informations sur les écosystèmes
pas dérangés. Les caractéristiques des forêts, les terrains
parés mais pas cultivés et les labours fournissent les informations pour estimer les effets de l'agriculture sur les sols
"Gray-Brown Podzolic" et "Brown Forest." On peut analyser des
évènements historiques, des methodes agricoles, des modèles du
peuplement et des agglomérations urbaines et puis voir l'impact
humain sur le paysage naturel.

En étudiant les strates, qui consistent en moraine, on peut
voir les profils du sol distinctifs qui représentent l'âge des
strates et les modifications qui résultent de l'agriculture.
On a pris et a décrit des échantillons de "Leaside Till" qui
consistent en le dolomite, le calcaire, le schiste, le granite
et le gneiss, et une région du climat et de la végétation de la
moyenne latitude qu'on trouve aux emplacements qui sont hauts et
bien évacués.

Les sols naturels sont en grande partie des "Alfisols" qui
forment aux sommets des collines où on trouve les horizons
"illuvial argillic." Les profils sont bien aérés et l'horizon B
contient du sol argileux à peu près de quarante-cinq pour-cent.

Cet horizon du sol se perd dans des sols des forêts, des sols
pas cultivés et des sols qu'on a labourés. Les types et les
ordres des horizons du sol entre la forêt, l'écotone et les
régions cultivées et le rapport chimique ne changent pas. Les
systèmes des sols où on a labouré et a atomisé un insecticide
contiennent plus d'argile en surface et moins de la matière
organique. Les informations indiquent que les minéraux d'argile
et le terreau absorbent un peu de "DDT, DDD, DDE, dieldrin, et
atrazine" mais que les matériaux toxiques dégradent plus vite
dans les sols cultivés.

AUSZUG

Die natürliche Umgebung südzentral Ontarios ist
ein Produkt der Quartärvergletscherung (Quaternary
glaciations), die ein dünnes Gesteingeschiebe auf
Muttergestein der Ordovizium und Silurzeit ablagerte
und weiterhin bestimmt wurde von associated interstadial and interglacial lacustrine)Binnensee-
Süsswasserablagerungen), fluvial und Deltasedimenten,
postglacial fluvial, aeolian (äolischem Gestein), sowie
weiter bestimmt durch Verwitterung und Erneuerung des
Vegetationsvorgangs (revegetation process). Eine
Analyse der geringen noch bestehenden laubwechselnden
Waldbestände (mixed-decidious forest ecosystems)im
östlichen Toronto und in den Städten Markham und Pick=
ering verschafft grundlegende Informationen über das
Wesen ungestörter Waldbodenvegetationsoberflächenformen
(forest-soil-vegetation-landform-systems). Die Eigen=
schaften und Wesenart der Waldbestände (forest ecotone
sites), der unbestellten sowie geernteten Felder ver=
schaffen die Daten für eine Bewertung der Auswirkung
landwirtschaftlicher Praxis auf Podsolboden (Gray-Brown
Podzolic) und Waldboden (brown forest soil systems).
Eine Analyse dokumentierter geschichtlicher Ereignisse,
der landwirtschaftlichen Praxis, des Ansiedlungs- und
Verstädtlichungsprozesses verschafft eine ausführlichere
Einsicht des menschlichen Einflusses auf die Landschafts=
natur.

Gesteinstratigraphische Einheiten (rock-stratigraphic units) aus Geschiebelehm (till)bestehend enthalten
deutliche Bodenprofile die dem Alter der Einheit ent=
sprechen sowie dem Grad der Änderung durch landwirt=
schaftliche Praxis, welches zu ersehen ist an der
äusseren Gesteinstruktur (field morphology), den struktur
und organischen Profilen (textural and organic profiles),
der Tonmineralogie (clay mineralogy), sowie an chemi=
scher Bodenanalyse (soil-chemical analysis) und Schäd=
lingsbekämpfungsmittelrückständen (pesticide residue).
Bodenproben representativer Ablagerungen von Leaside
Till wurden beschrieben. Sie bestehen zum grossen Teil
aus Dolomit, Kalkstein, Schiefergestein sowie aus Granit
und Gneiss, und enstammen einem Gebiet mittlerer Breite
mit feuchtem mikrothermalischem Klima und Vegetation
(an area of middle-latitude humid microthermal climate
and vegetation) mit guter Entwässerung, situiert auf
topographisch hochgelegenen Plätzen.

Der natürliche unbestellte Boden besteht meist aus
Alfisols die sich auf Hügelspitzen bilden wo dünner
spätpleistozäner und holozäner Löss eingespülte Ton=
horizonte begräbt (loess buries illuvial argillic horizons). Die Profile sind gut aufgelockert und die kalk=

haltige Tonansammlung in eingespülten B Horizonten
(illuvial B horizons) erreicht 45 Prozent. Von den
Tonmineralien in der Muttersubstanz ist Montmorillonit-
Illit vorrängig und verwittert dann zu Chlorit, Kaolinit
und Halloysit.

Dieser bodenstratigraphische Horizont vereinigt
sich mit dem Waldboden (forest ecotone soils), dem
Boden freier unbestellter Lagen, mit Boden in bestell=
ten Lagen von zweitem Wuchs und mit gepflügtem Boden.
Die Typen und Reihenfolgen des Bodenhorizonts bleiben
gleich zwischem Wald, ecotone und freien Lagen, und
das chemische Verhältnis der Tonmineralien bleibt auch
gleich. Bodensysteme beeinflusst durch Pflügen und den
Gebrauch von Insektenvertilgungsmittel und Unkraut=
vertilgungsmittel haben eine höhere Ansammlung von Ton
in der Erdoberfläche, eine geringere Menge organischer
Materie und im ganzen ein reduziertes Kohlenstoff-
Nitrogen Verhältnis. Die Daten weisen darauf hin, dass
Tonminerale und Humus DDT, DDD, DDE, Dieldrin sowie
atrazine in kleinen Mengen absorbieren, aber die
meisten giftigen Materien degradieren in schnellerem
Mass in gepflügtem Boden.

SUMARIO

El ambiente natural del sector Sud-Central de Ontario es un producto de las glaciaciones Cuaternarias que depositaran finas láminas de acarreos en roca sólida en los períodos Silurianos y Ordovicianos; interstadial e interglacial lacustres relacionados, depósitos fluviales y deltaicos; y procesos post-glaciales fluviales, aeolian -- llevados por el viento --, desgaste por la acción atmosférica y revegetación. El análisis de uno de los pocos lechos existentes en los ecosistemas forestales efímero-mezclados (hojas caducas), al oriente de Ontario y en las ciudades de Markham y Pickering, proveen información básica sobre la naturaleza de los sistemas forestales-suelos-vegetación-formaciones de suelos que permanecen sin alteración. La naturaleza y el carácter de locales forestales ecotonos, locales limpios y sin cultivar, y de campos arados proveen información para evaluar los efectos de los procesos agrícolas en los sistemas de suelos Gray-Brown Podzolic y Brown Forest. El análisis de la documentación de eventos históricos, procesos agrícolas, normas de colonización y procesos de urbanización, proveen un panorama amplio del impacto humano en el boscaje natural.

Unidades de rocas estratigráficas formadas por materias de cultivo acarrean los perfiles característicos de los suelos que representan la edad de la unidad y el grado de modificación ocurrido a causa de métodos agrícolas y determinados por la morfología del terreno, los perfiles orgánicos y de textura, la mineralogía de la arcilla, el análisis químico del suelo y el residuo de los pesticidas. Se probó y describió suelos de depósitos obtenidos en el Leaside Till, los cuales estaban compuestos, en su mayoría, de dolomita, piedra caliza, arcilla esquistosa, granítico, litologías gnéisicas, y una área de latitud media, de clima húmedo micro-termal y vegetación y en sitios topográficamente elevados y con buen drenaje.

Los suelos naturales no-cultivados son, generalmente, de formación Alfisols y se encuentran en las cimas de cerros donde una fina lámina de arcilla calcárea (loess) del late-Pleistoceno y Holoceno entierra horizontes de sales solubles y partículas minerales (illuvial) y de tipo arcilloso (argillic). Los perfiles son bien gaseosos y la acumulación de arcilla en los horizontes en el illuvial llega al 45 por ciento. Los minerales arcillosos en la materia original están dominados por illite-montmorillonite que se convierte en clorita, kaolinita -- terra alba --, y halloysite en el solum.

Este horizonte de suelo-estratigráfico se une a los suelos forestales ecotone, suelos en locales limpios y sin cultivar, suelos en áreas de cultivo de segunda vegetación (crecimiento) y suelos arados. Los tipos y sucesiones de los horizontes del suelo permanecen igual en el bosque, el ecotone y en las áreas despejadas y las relaciones químico-minerales de la arcilla son similares. Los sistemas de suelo que han sido expuestos (influenciados) al arado, y la aplicación de insecticidas y herbicidas contienen una acumulación mayor de arcilla en la superficie y una menor de materia orgánica y, en su totalidad, una reducción en la proporción (ratio) carbón-nitrógeno. Los datos indican que los minerales de arcilla y humus absorben el DDT, DDD, DDE, dieldrin y atrazine en pequeñas cantidades pero la mayoría de los materiales tóxicos se degradan en proporción más rápida en los suelos arados.

REFERENCES

Albrecht, W.A., 1971, Physical, chemical and biochemical changes in the soil community, in Detwyler, Thomas R., ed., Man's Impact on Environment: N.Y., McGraw-Hill, p. 395-418.

Barthel, W.F., et al., 1966, Surface hydrology and pesticides, in Bloodworth, M.E., et al., eds., Pesticides and Their Effects on Soils and Water, A.S.A. Special Publication No. 8: Madison, Wisc., Amer. Soc. Agron., p. 128-144.

Birkeland, P.W., 1969, Quaternary paleoclimatic implications of soil-clay mineral distribution in a Sierra Nevada-Great Basin transect: Jour. Geol., v. 77, p. 289-302.

Bonis, R.R., 1965, A History of Scarborough: Scarborough, Ontario, Scarborough Public Library.

Bouma, J., 1969, Microstructure and Stability of Two Sandy Loam Soils With Different Soil Management: Wageningen, Center for Agricultural Publishing and Documentation, 100 p.

Bouyoucos, G.J., 1962, Hydrometer method improved for making particle size analyses of soils: Agron. Jour., v. 54, p. 464-465.

Bower, C.A., and Wilcox, L.V., 1965, Soluble salts, in Black, C.A., ed., Methods of Soil Analysis, Part 2: Madison, Wisc., Amer. Soc. Agron., p. 933-951.

Bowman, Irene, 1974, The Draper Site: White Pine succession on an abandoned Late Prehistoric Iroquoian maize field, in Konrad, V.A., et al., eds., North Pickering Archaeology, Research Report No. 4: Toronto, Ontario Ministry of Natural Resources.

Bremner, J.R., 1965, Toral nitrogen, in Black, C.A., ed., Methods of Soil Analysis, Part 2.: Madison, Wisc., Amer. Soc. Agron., p. 1149-1176.

Brown, D.M., et al., 1968, The Climate of Southern Ontario, Climatological Studies No. 5, Department of Transport, Meteorological Branch: Ottawa, Queen's Printer.

Brown, G., 1972, Other minerals, in Brown, G., ed., The X-ray
    Identification and Crystal Structures of Clay Miner-
    als: London, Mineralogical Society, 544 p.

Bureau of Municipal Research, 1974, Control of Urban Growth,
    B.M.R. Comment No. 148: Toronto, Bureau of Municipal
    Research.

Butzer, K.W., 1974, Accelerated soil erosion: a problem of
    man-land relationships, in Manners, I.R., and Mikesell,
    M.W., eds., Perspectives on Environment: Washington,
    D.C., Commission on College Geography, Association
    American Geographers, p. 57-78.

Careless, J.M.S., 1967, The Union of the Canadas: Toronto,
    McClelland and Stewart.

City of Toronto Planning Board, 1974, Pickering Impact Study
    Summary Report, v. 1: Toronto, Toronto Planning Board.

Coleman, A.P., 1932, The Pleistocene of the Toronto Region:
    Toronto, Ontario Department Mines, v. 41, pt. 7.

COLUC (Central Ontario Lakeshore Urbanized Complex), 1974,
    Report to the Advisory Committee on Urban and Regional
    Planning of the Central Ontario Lakeshore Urban Com-
    plex Task Force: Toronto, Ontario Government.

Dale, Thomas and Carter, V.G., 1955, Topsoil and Civilization:
    Norman, Okla., Univ. of Oklahoma Press.

Day, P., 1965, Particle fractionation and particle-size
    analysis, in Black, C.A., ed., Methods of Soil Analy-
    sis, Part 1: Madison, Wisc., Amer. Soc. Agron., p.
    545-567.

Dreimanis, A., and Terasmae, J., 1958, Stratigraphy of Wiscon-
    sin glacial deposits of Toronto area, Ontario: Geol.
    Assoc. Canada Proc., v. 10, p. 119-136.

Fiskell, J.G.A., and Calvert, D.V., 1975, Effects of deep
    tillage, lime incorporation, and drainage on chemical
    properties of spodosol profiles: Soil Sci., v. 120,
    no. 2, p. 132-139.

Fleck, E.E., 1949, The action of ultraviolet light on DDT:
    Jour. Amer. Chem. Soc., v. 71, p. 1034-1036.

_____, and Haller, H., 1946, Stability of DDT and related compounds: Jour. Amer. Chem. Soc., v. 68, p. 142-143.

Folk, R.L., 1968, Petrology of Sedimentary Rocks: Austin, Texas, Hamphill Press, 170 p.

Freed, V.H., 1966, Chemistry of herbicides, in Bloodworth, M.E., et al., eds., Pesticides and Their Effects on Soils and Water, A.S.A. Special Publication No. 8: Madison, Wisc., Amer. Soc. Agron., p. 25-43.

Gentilcore, R.L., 1963, The beginnings of settlement in the Niagara Peninsula (1782-1792): Canadian Geographer, v. 7, p. 78.

Gilyarov, M.S., 1942, Comparative abundance of soil fauna in dark colored and in podzolic soils: Pochvovedenie, no. 9 and 10.

Government of Ontario, 1970, Design for Development: The Toronto Centred Region: Toronto, Queen's Printer.

_____, 1971, Design for Development: The Toronto Centred Region, Status Report: Toronto, Queen's Printer.

Greenwald, Michelle, 1973, The historical complexities of Pickering, Markham, Scarborough and Uxbridge, in North Pickering Community Development Project: Toronto, Ontario, Ministry of Treasury, Economics and Intergovernmental Affairs.

Grim, R., 1968, Clay Mineralogy: N.Y., McGraw-Hill, 596 p.

Haller, H., et al., 1945, The chemical composition of technical DDT: Jour. Amer. Chem. Soc., v. 67, p. 1591.

Heidenreich, C., 1963, The Indian occupance of Huronia: Canadian Geographer, v. 7, no. 3, p. 131-144.

_____, 1972, The Huron: a brief ethnography: Toronto, York University, Dept. of Geography, Discussion Paper No. 6.

Hewitt, D.F., and Freeman, E.B., 1972, Rocks and Minerals of Ontario: Toronto, Ontario Dept. Mines and Northern Affairs, 135 p.

Hoffman, D.W., and Richards, N.R., 1955, Soil Survey of York County, Report No. 19, Ontario Soil Survey: Guelph, Ontario, Canada Dept. Agriculture, 104 p.

Innis, H.A., 1971, A History of the Canadian Pacific Railways: Toronto, University of Toronto Press.

Jenny, H., 1941, Factors of Soil Formation: N.Y., McGraw-Hill, 281 p.

_____, 1961, Derivation of state factor equations of soils and ecosystems: Proc. Soil Sci. Soc. Amer., v. 25, p. 385-388.

Jones, R.L., 1946, History of Agriculture in Ontario, 1613-1880: Toronto, University of Toronto Press.

Kachinskii, N.A., 1927, Freezing, thawing and moisture content of soil in winter, under forest and on fields: Moskva.

Karrow, P.F., 1967, Pleistocene geology of the Scarborough Area, Geological Report No. 46: Toronto, Ont. Dept. Mines, 108 p.

Kaufman, D.D., 1966, Structure of pesticides and decomposition by microorganisms, in Bloodworth, M.E., et al., eds., Pesticides and Their Effects on Soils and Water, A.S.A. Spec. Publ. No. 8: Madison, Wisc., Amer. Soc. Agron., p. 85-94.

Kondrat'yev, A.A. and Gritsenko, V.V., 1971, Changes produced by deep tillage in the agronomical properties of sod-podzolic soils: Soviet Soil Science, v. 3, p. 286-294.

Konrad, V.A., and Ross, W.A., 1974, An archaeological survey for the North Pickering Project, in Konrad, V.A., et al., eds., North Pickering Archaeology, Research Report No. 4: Toronto, Ontario Ministry of Natural Resources.

Kuchler, A.W., 1964, Potential Natural Vegetation of the Conterminous U.S., Spec. Pub. No. 36: N.Y., American Geographical Society, 116 p.

Levin, F.I., 1969, Improvement of Sod-Podzolic Soils by Cultivation: Jerusalem, Israel Program Scientific Translation, 109 p.

Liberty, B.A., 1953, Stratigraphy and paleontology of Lake
    Simcoe district, Ontario (Ph.D. Dissert.): Toronto,
    University of Toronto.

_____, 1955, Studies of the Ordovician system in
    Central Ontario: Proc. Geol. Assoc. Canada, v. 7
    (Part 1), p. 139-147.

_____, 1964, Upper Ordovician stratigraphy of the
    Toronto area, in Guidebook, Geology of Central Ontario:
    Amer. Assoc. Pet. Geol., p. 43-53.

_____, 1967, Paleozoic stratigraphy of the Kingston
    area, Ontario, in Jenness, S.E., ed., Guidebook,
    Geology of parts of Eastern Ontario and Western Quebec:
    Geol. Assoc. Canada, p. 167-182.

Low, A.J., 1972, The effect of cultivation on the structure
    and other physical characteristics of grassland and
    arable soils (1945-1970): Jour. Soil Sci., v. 23,
    no. 4, p. 363-380.

_____, 1973, Soil structure and crop yield: Jour. Soil
    Sci., v. 24, no. 2, p. 249-259.

Mahaney, W.C., 1974, Soil stratigraphy and genesis of Neo-
    glacial deposits in the Arapaho and Henderson cirques,
    central Colorado Front Range, in Mahaney, W.C., ed.,
    Quaternary Environments: Proceedings of a Symposium:
    Toronto, Geographical Monographs, No. 5, p. 197-240.

_____, and Fahey, B.D., 1976, Late-Quaternary soil
    stratigraphy of the Colorado Front Range, in Mahaney,
    W.C., ed., The Quaternary Stratigraphy of North Amer-
    ica: Stroudsburg, Penna., Dowden, Hutchinson and
    Ross, 608 p.

Mehra, O.P., and Jackson, M.L., 1960, Iron oxide removal from
    soils and clays by a dithionite citrate system buf-
    fered with sodium bicarbonate, Natl. Conf. on Clays
    and Clay Minerals, 1958: London, Pergamon Press, p.
    317-327.

Metcalf, R.L., 1955, Organic Insecticides: N.Y., Interscience,
    392 p.

Metropolitan Toronto Planning Board, 1959, The Official Plan
    of the Metropolitan Toronto Planning Area: Toronto,
    Municipality of Metropolitan Toronto.

_____, 1974, Preliminary Impressions of the Urban Structure: To 1971: Toronto, Research and Transportation Divisions, 117 p.

Mitchell, J., 1950, The Settlement of York County: Toronto: Municipal Corporation of the County of York.

MTARTS (Metropolitan Toronto and Region Transportation Study), 1967, Metropolitan Toronto and Region Transportation Study: Choices for a growing region: Toronto, Queen's Printer.

Olding, A.B., et al., 1956, Soil Survey of Ontario County, Report No. 23, Ontario Soil Survey: Guelph, Ontario, Canada Dept. Agriculture, 60 p.

Olsen, S.R., and Dean, L.A., 1965, Phosphorus, in Black, C.A., ed., Methods of Soil Analysis, Part 2: Madison, Wisc., Amer. Soc. Agron., p. 1035-1048.

Ostry, R.C., 1962, An analysis of some tills in Scarborough Township and vicinity (M.A. Thesis): Toronto, University of Toronto.

Peech, M.L., et al., 1947, Methods of soil analyses for soil fertility investigations: U.S.D.A. Circ. 757, p. 25.

Phillips, D.W., and McCulloch, J.A.W., 1972, The Climate of the Great Lakes Basin, Climatological Studies No. 20: Ottawa, Environment Canada.

Regional Municipality of York, 1972, An Interim Policy on Rural-Residential Development: Newmarket, Ontario, Regional Municipality of York.

_____, 1974, Physical Base of York Region, Regional Official Plan, Technical Appendix 2: Newmarket, Ont., Regional Municipality of York.

Richards, N.R., 1961, The soils of Southern Ontario, in Legget, R.F., ed., Soils in Canada, Toronto, University of Toronto Press, p. 174-182.

Richardson, A.H., 1956, Rouge, Duffin, Highland, Petticoat (RDHP) Conservation Report: Toronto, Ontario Dept. Planning and Development.

Rode, A.A., 1970, Podzol-Forming Process: Jerusalem, Israel Program Scientific Translations, 387 p.

Rowe, J.S., 1972, Forest Regions of Canada, Canadian Forestry Service: Ottawa, Environment Canada.

Russell, E.W., 1955, Soil Conditions and Plant Growth: London, Longmans, 688 p.

Schollenberger, C.J., and Simon, R.H., 1945, Determination of exchange capacity and exchangeable bases in soils-ammonium acetate method: Soil Sci., v. 59, p. 13-24.

Soane, B.D. and Pidgeon, J.D., 1975, Tillage requirement in relation to soil physical properties: Soil Sci., v. 119, no. 5, p. 376-384.

Soil Survey Staff, 1951, Soil Survey Manual: Washington, D.C., U.S. Gov't Printing Office, 503 p.

_____, 1960, Soil Classification, 7th Approximation, Soil Conservation Service: Washington, D.C., U.S. Gov't Printing Office, 265 p.

Stevens, G.R., 1962, Canadian National Railways: Towards the Inevitable, 1896-1922: Toronto, Clarke Irwin.

Stobbe, P.C., 1961, Characteristics and genesis of podzol soils, in Legget, R.F., ed., Soil in Canada; Toronto, University of Toronto Press, p. 158-164.

_____, and Wright, J.R., 1959, Modern concepts of the genesis of podzols: Proc. Soil Sci. Soc. Amer., v. 23, p. 161-164.

Talbert, R.E., and Fletchall, O.H., 1965, The adsorption of some s-triazines in soils: Weeds, v. 13, p. 46-52.

Terasmae, J., 1960, A palynological study of Pleistocene interglacial beds at Toronto, Ontario: Ottawa, Geol. Surv. Canada, Bull. 56, p. 24-40.

_____, 1975, Notes on Pleistocene stratigraphy of the Toronto area, in Mahaney, W.C., ed. Quaternary Stratigraphy Symposium, Abstracts-with-Program, p. 91-121.

Walden, F.A., and Griffiths, M., 1974, A biological survey of the North Pickering Site and Toronto II Airport Site: Toronto, Ontario Ministry of Housing.

Walkley, A., and Black, I.A., 1934, An examination of the Degtjareff method for determining soil organic matter, and a proposed modification of the chromic acid titration method: Soil Sci., v. 37, p. 29-38.

Watt, A., 1954, Correlation of the Pleistocene geology as seen in the subway with that of the Toronto region, Canada: Geol. Assoc. Canada Proc., v. 6, p. 69-82.

_____, 1955, Pleistocene geology and groundwater resources of the township of North York, York County: Toronto, Ont. Dept. Mines.

Weber, J.B., and Weed, S.B., 1974, Effects of soil on the biological activity of pesticides, in Guenzi, W.D., ed., Pesticides in Soil and Water: Madison, Wisc., Soil Sci. Soc. Amer., p. 223-256.

Whittig, L.D., 1965, X-ray diffraction techniques for mineral identification and mineralogical composition, in Black, C.A., ed., Methods of Soil Analysis, Part 1: Madison, Wisc., Amer. Soc. Agron., p. 671-696.

Wood, W.R., 1911, Past Years in Pickering: Toronto, William Briggs.